What Readers Say

"Loved the *No B.S. Business Book*[...] resources department type inside[...] own company 11 months ago. Yo[...] HRD, I would know how to manage people [...] into a wall with my most important staff member and YOUR advice and suggestions on how to approach this situation pulled me out of a very difficult period."

—Kim Bechtel, The Humanix Company

"There is more truth about the entrepreneurial experience in this book than in an entire MBA program."

—Dr. Herb True, Adjunct Professor, Notre Dame University

"Thanks to the principles you present in this book, I have built a business to suit me, that actually works better and brings in more money when I'm not there than when I am!"

—Jerry Jones, CEO, Jerry Jones Direct

Media Raves about the *No B.S. Business Book* and Its Author

INC. magazine included the first edition of this book in its list of "100 Best Business Books' (1994). Here are a few other media comments:

"The *No B.S. Business Book* delivers hard-nosed advice for real-life entrepreneurs who must meet payrolls, satisfy customers, and battle bankers and bureaucrats."

—*Houston Business Journal*

"….there are even paragraphs of your writing that are as good as Tom Wolfe's. And I should know. I published an original 7,500 word piece by Mr. Wolfe."

—Rich Karlgaard, Contributing Editor/Publisher, *Forbes Magazine*, Forbes.com

N🐂B.S.
BUSINESS
SUCCESS

N⊘B.S.
BUSINESS
SUCCESS

THE ULTIMATE
NO HOLDS BARRED
KICK BUTT
TAKE NO PRISONERS
TOUGH & SPIRITED
GUIDE

Dan Kennedy

Entrepreneur.
Press

Editorial Director: Jere L. Calmes
Cover Design: David Shaw
Production and Composition: Eliot House Productions

This publication is designed to provide accurate and authoritative information in regard to the subject matter covered. It is sold with the understanding that the publisher is not engaged in rendering legal, accounting or other professional services. If legal advice or other expert assistance is required, the services of a competent professional person should be sought.

Library of Congress Cataloging-in-Publication Data
Kennedy, Dan S., 1954–
No B.S. business success: the ultimate no holds barred kick butt, take no prisoners, tough and spirited guide/by Dan Kennedy
p.   cm.
ISBN 1-932531-10-6
1. Selling. 2. Success in business. I. Title: Ultimate no holds barred kick butt, take no prisoners, and make tons of money guide. II. Title.
HF5438.25.K473 2004
658.85—dc22   2004045554

Printed in Canada
09 08 07 06 05 04   10 9 8 7 6 5 4 3

Contents

Foreword
by Brian Tracy

Y ou are about to get into a business championship fight. In this book, you will be knocked around, and many of your most cherished ideas will get punched and stomped on. Like a roller coaster, your stomach will drop, and you might have trouble breathing. But don't worry, you'll arrive safely at the other end.

In my years as a consultant and business speaker, I've written 28 books, translated into 20 languages, and produced more than 300 audio and video learning programs. I have a good understanding of the importance and value of good business ideas.

My friend Dan Kennedy is unique, a genius in many ways. I have always admired his ability to see the vital truths in any business and to state these realities with straight language and clear definitions.

Dan has written a timeless book, with ideas, insights, and methods you can use immediately to get better, faster business results.

His approach is direct. His ideas are controversial. His ability to get results for his clients is unchallenged. When you read, learn, and apply what you discover in the pages ahead, your business life and your income will change forever.

Put up your mental tray tables. Put on your conceptual seatbelts. You are entering an area of considerable turbulence. But you will come out of this experience a better businessperson than you ever have been. You will arrive at your destination of business success and profitability faster than you ever thought possible.

Good luck, and *bon voyage*!

—Brian Tracy

Brian Tracy is one of America's most sought after and popular professional speakers, author of dozens of business books (including *Turbo Strategy: 21 Ways to Transform Your Business*), and a visionary thinker about business trends, opportunities, and strategies. Learn more about him at www.briantracy.com.

Preface

Just a spoonful of sugar helps the medicine go down.

—R. SHERMAN, FROM *MARY POPPINS*

Welcome to what I sincerely hope is the most truthful, blunt, straightforward, non-sugarcoated, no pabulum, no holds barred, no-nonsense, no B.S. book you have ever read on succeeding as an entrepreneur.

I wrote the first edition of this book back in 1993, and since then, I've personally heard from thousands of readers from all over the world. You saw a few of their comments on the opening pages of this book. It struck a chord with entrepreneurs; the chord of authenticity. No college classroom theory, no baloney. Real world truths from somebody who succeeds day in, day out, as an entrepreneur, working without a net. Since then, a lot has happened in my life, business and personal. For example, I've sold two businesses I built up; walked away from a very important and lucrative nine-year business relationship; made well-planned, continual, evolutionary changes in my other businesses; gone through a divorce after 22 years of marriage; been diagnosed diabetic; and more. I'm pleased to report I'm happier than I've been in many years and am living the life I set out to live.

Anyway, all these changes, new experiences, and lessons I've learned from my clients certainly warranted a complete updating of this book.

It is a personal book, me talking straight with you, as if I was consulting with you and as if we were sitting around at the end of the day on my deck, watching the sunset, enjoying adult beverages, and just hanging out. Because it is personal, along the way I'll be telling you quite a bit about me and about my business life—past, present, and future. None of this is about bragging. I have no need for that or interest in doing it. What I share, I tell you so that you understand the basis for the advice and opinions I dispense.

I have occasionally been introduced as The Professor of Harsh Reality. This does NOT mean I'm negative. If anything, I'm one of the most optimistic, positive-minded people you'll ever meet. However, I do not believe in confusing positive thinking with fantasy. And the word *optimism*, like many words in our perplexing English language, has more than one meaning. There's a mammoth difference between earned, deserved, justified optimism and wild-eyed, blue-sky, stubborn optimism.

I've discovered that I'm most successful when I have a firm grip on what is and least successful when caught wrestling with what ought to be.

In this book, I've tried to share, from my 25-plus years of entrepreneurial adventure, what *is*. Not what *should be* or what is only in theoretical books, classrooms, or seminar rooms.

If You Are Already in Business for Yourself

This book will help you go forward more astutely, efficiently, productively, and confidently. I think you'll also catch yourself nodding as you go along, saying to yourself, "This guy has been where I live." Sometimes there is value in just finding out you're not alone! The very first "success education" that I was ever exposed to was a set of recordings by Earl Nightingale titled *Lead the Field*, that I listened to when I was in my early teens. In those tapes, Nightingale gave me badly needed permission to violate the norms I saw around me, with his dramatic statement:

> *If you have no successful example to follow in whatever endeavor you choose, you may simply look at what everyone else around you is doing and do the opposite, because—THE MAJORITY IS ALWAYS WRONG.*

That may not be a precise, verbatim quote; but it is what I recall and have stored in my subconscious as a primary guiding principle. This leads to my strategy of deliberately questioning all industry norms, deliberately violating most of them, and encouraging my clients to do the same. It also led to my coining of the term "Mediocre Majority" to succinctly describe the vast undistinguished middle of any industry or profession. Anyway, Earl said a lot of things I had been thinking but had never heard anyone validate, and that gave me a great boost of confidence and conviction. Maybe some of my words, here, will do the same for you.

Most entrepreneurs tell me that the feeling they get from this book make them instantly eager to share it with other entrepreneurs. Please do so! If you want some place to send them, refer to www.nobsbooks.com.

If You Have Not Yet Started in Business but Intend To

This book might scare you off. If it does, consider it a favor; you're too easily spooked to succeed anyway. The entrepreneurial arena is no place for the timid, nervous, or easily worried to come and play.

If it doesn't scare you off, it will help you avoid many pitfalls and problems and help you cope with those that can't be avoided. It will not cover the basics. There are plenty of books out there on the basics, and we're not going to cover the same ground all over again. This is not a how-to-start-a-small-business book. This is a go-for-the-jugular success book.

As I said earlier, I am not a fuzzy-headed academic, pocket-protector-and-wingtip-shoes accountant, or other theorist, although plenty of these pretenders write business books. I'm also not a retired authority who runs a business in my memory. I've been on the firing line meeting a payroll, battling the bankers and bureaucrats, struggling to satisfy customers, and solving real business problems. Over years, I've arrived at a point where my own business is engineered to meet all my lifestyle preferences—for example, only one employee, in a distant office, not under-foot; no set hours; no unscheduled phone calls. But still, I deal with clients and vendors and real business life just like you do. I also work very hands-on with clients in a wide variety of busi-nesses, as well as being "the consultant to the consultants"—I advise more than 50 different leading marketing and business consultants, each exclusively serving a different business or pro-fessional niche, in direct, hands-on relationships with more than one million small business owners. I want you to know this because I think it makes this book more valuable to you.

I'll never forget taking over a company with 43 employees, never having managed more than two people in my life. I grabbed every management book I could get my paws on and sucked up all the experts' advice. Then, after a couple of months of getting my brains beat in every day by my employees, I started to look critically at the credentials of those "expert" authors.

Most of them had never—I repeat, never—managed a workforce. These geniuses spewing out creative management, nonmanipulative management, Japanese management, open-door management, and everything-else management wouldn't have survived a week in the real world. I resent those authors to this day. And it's a shame that a lot of college kids get that management theory, that is, fantasy sold to them as reality. So, I chucked all their books, rolled up my sleeves, used my common sense, and started finding out what really works and what doesn't.

Ever since then, I look at every new business book with suspicion. Most won't pass muster because most can't pass the real-experience test. I was originally motivated to write this book largely because reading most of the other books written for and sold to entrepreneurs turned my stomach.

I also want you to know that there are a lot more things I haven't got a clue about than there are things I understand; in this book, I have not dealt with any of the many things I'm in the dark about. Everything in here is based on my own expensive experience. It may not be right. You may not agree with it. But at least you should know that I didn't swipe it out of somebody else's book, give it a jazzy new psychobabble name, and pass it off as a new miracle tonic.

It's about Getting Rich

I also know you can't eat philosophy. So, although there is a lot of my own philosophy in this book, its primary job is to show you how to make more money then you ever imagined possible, faster than you can believe possible. This is a book about getting rich. If that offends you, please put this book back on the shelf or take it back to the store and get a refund. Spend your money on milk and cookies instead. You'll be happier. In fact, I'd like to quickly clear up a big misconception about what being an entrepreneur and owning and building a business is all about. The purpose is *not* to employ people, *not* to do social good, *not* to pay taxes. A lot of liberals think those are the purposes of business. Nuts to them. The purpose of being an entrepreneur is to get really, really rich, and reward yourself for taking on all the risk and responsibility with exactly the kind of life and lifestyle you want. Facilitating that is the sole aim of this book.

Before getting into the "meat," on the next few pages, you'll find a brief description of my business activities past and present and my current business in the back of the book beginning on page 247. I think you'll benefit more from the book if you understand where I'm coming from; however, you can choose to skip these pages if you like and jump right to Chapter 1. Your choice.

I'd like to explain the *Mary Poppins* quote at the top of this Preface. *Mary Poppins* was one of the first movies I was taken to see in a theater as a child. I watched it just the other night on cable TV and enjoyed it thoroughly. If you've seen it, you can probably call up the scene of Julie Andrews and the children singing the "just a spoonful of sugar helps the medicine go down" song. It's a lovely thought. (Or as she would say, "loverly.") In real business life, however, the emotional need for spoonfuls of sugar is very dangerous. How well you can take medicine—deal with reality—has a great deal to do with how successful you are as an entrepreneur.

There's a legendary book by Napoleon Hill I hope you've read, titled *Think and Grow Rich*. In that book, he enumerates 17 success principles adhered to in common by the hundreds of history's greatest entrepreneurial achievers he studied, interviewed and worked with, such as Andrew Carnegie, Henry Ford, Thomas Edison, and so on. Of the 17 principles, the one everybody seems to like the least and ignore the most is "accurate thinking." I believe it to be the most important one. So this book, my book, is heavy on that principle. It is medicine without the accompaniment of sugar.

Finally, let me say that, when I graduated high school, my parents were flat broke. I started with no family money. I didn't step into a family business. No one handed me anything on a silver platter. At age 49, I am semi-retiring, a multimillionaire, free to live precisely as I choose, indulging my interest in horse racing. It was all made possible through the kind of thinking, attitudes, habits, and strategies I've laid out in this book. I have been blunt, forthright, and held nothing back.

With that said, I still hope you not only profit from this book, but enjoy reading it. And I welcome your comments, thoughts, or questions. You can communicate with me directly by fax, 602-269-3113.

—Dan S. Kennedy

Other Notes from the Author

1. For those of you who are gender or political correctness sensitive, an explanation to head off letters: I have used "he," "him," etc. throughout the book rather than awkwardly saying "he or she," "him or her." I do not mean this as slight to women, only as a convenience. I'm not getting paid by the word.

2. In most instances, I've been able to use the names of actual companies and individuals and the details of actual case

histories and examples. In a few cases, individuals' names have been withheld on request.

3. The first edition of this book was published in 1993 by Self-Counsel Press. A revised and updated edition was published in 1995. This edition, published by Entrepreneur Press, preserved approximately half of the original text with only statistics or time-altered information revised. About 50% of the book is brand-new material.

CHAPTER 1

The Decision and
Determination to Succeed

Men are anxious to improve their circumstances,
but are unwilling to improve themselves.
They therefore remain bound.

—JAMES ALLEN, AS A MAN THINKETH

Contrary to a great many textbook assertions, having the best product, the better mousetrap, a whiz-bang new idea, the top location, the best market, the smartest accountant, the neatest bookkeeping system, a ton of capital—or all of them together—does not ensure success. On the other hand, having the worst product, a mediocre mousetrap, a silly idea, a bad location, a weak market, an accountant who can't count, a shoe box and paper bag bookkeeping system, or no money—or all of these things together—does not ensure failure.

I have seen people succeed under the most improbable conditions. I've also seen people who have everything going for them still manage to screw it up. In all of these cases, it's the person making the difference. That's why there really are no business successes or failures; there are people successes and people failures.

Entrepreneurial Success Is Mostly a Matter of Decision

A partnership, friendship, intimate relationship, or marriage that succeeds or fails, a book that gets written or remains a jumble of notes in a drawer, the garage that gets cleaned out Saturday or put off until next week—these are all the result of decision and determination to make the decision right. Making the *right decisions* is often a lot less important than determining to make your *decisions right*. Only by making a decision and acting on it can you get into action and move forward. By waiting to make only

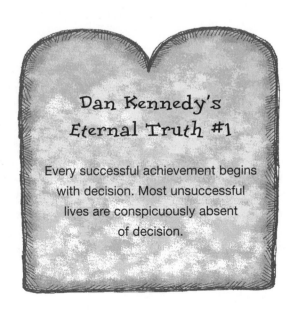

Dan Kennedy's
Eternal Truth #1

Every successful achievement begins
with decision. Most unsuccessful
lives are conspicuously absent
of decision.

the perfect decisions, you remain inert and cannot move forward at all. To quote my friend, legendary ad man Gary Halbert, "Motion beats meditation."

Most people go through life making decisions by default, choosing only from narrow options dictated by others or by evolving circumstances. One millionaire friend of mine grew up in a very small town where, as he put it, there were two career options: working at the factory or raising pigs and chickens. With only a few exceptions, everybody he went to school and graduated with chose one of those two options.

I am often amused when I'm traveling and get asked what I do; when I describe my job as best I can, I often get the envious sigh, the gee-I-wish-I-could-do-that, and then the laundry list of complaints and dissatisfactions from my fellow traveler about present career or business or life. I'm amused because he apparently does not know he can change those circumstances by decision. Similarly, when I told fellow travelers that I lived in "sunny Phoenix" (where I lived for more than ten years), I'd often hear the envious sigh, the gee-I-wish-I-lived-there-instead-of-in-X, then the litany of unpleasant things about their home city. This amuses me because apparently they haven't noticed the highway signs in their town pointing the way out.

Successful entrepreneurs learn to be much more assertive, proactive, and creative in making decisions to change things as they prefer, to make things happen. If you are to succeed as an entrepreneur, you have to break free of your old reacting and responding mode and switch to the assertive, proactive mode. *You have to reject the entire idea of limited choices.*

As an entrepreneur, you need to reject every single piece of programming you've ever received about limited options or prerequisites for exercising certain options.

It's amazing how people spend their lives in prisons entirely of their own making, the key dangling right there in the lock, no jailer in sight.

I find it very hard to work up much sympathy for most of these "sad sacks." I remember listening to a 40-or-so-year-old guy working behind the counter at a neighborhood convenience store where I sometimes stop for coffee complaining loudly—even poetically—about his miserable job, low income, and lousy lot in life. I asked where he lived and which way he drove to work. After he answered, I asked if he'd noticed that every day, twice a day, he drove past the public library, a gigantic repository of free help for changing your career, your finances, your life. As you might guess, I might as well have been speaking Martian. If pressed, I assure you, he'd tell you he was too busy or too tired to read, or didn't like to read, or had bad eyesight when he was in school, or some other pitiful excuse. Pfui.

Just for example, you probably believe that certain options exist only for people with particular educations, licenses, or certifications. Sure, you can't just up and declare yourself a heart surgeon or airplane pilot. But you can certainly be a CEO, and you can certainly make as much money as you choose.

Here's a little jolt: one of the highest-paid marketing consultants and coaches working with Realtors, a man who is paid millions of dollars a year from real estate agents for his advice, has never been in real estate and does not have a real estate license. His name is Craig Forte, and he is a longtime client of mine. For four years, I had the largest business training company serving dentists and chiropractors, working with more than 10,000 doctors, but I am neither a DC nor DDS. I give you this one example as food for thought.

Warning: Your Entry Point to Entrepreneurship May Be a Handicap to Overcome

For many people, the decision to pursue the entrepreneurial lifestyle is the byproduct of an evolving dislike for their jobs, frustration with their bosses, or a sudden loss of employment. They may be downsized, Enroned, forced into early retirement, or just fed up enough one day to tell the boss to "take this job and shove it." The employees-turned-entrepreneurs out of default or disgust lug a lot of mental and emotional baggage with them. The habits, attitudes, and behaviors that work fine for the employee in the corporate bureaucratic environment do not work well at all in the entrepreneurial environment and must be left behind. The reason why so many new businesses fail is that the owners are unable to leave their old attitudes behind.

Personally, I've only held one job in my entire life, for one year, immediately out of high school. I secured a territory sales position with a national book publishing company, a job that was supposed to be for a college graduate with sales experience. I got it through a combination of bluster, white lies, and agreeing to work on "free trial" for three months—no pay, no company car. Although I excelled at the work itself, by year's end, I and my sales manager both agreed I was fundamentally unemployable. Thus, I became entrepreneurial.

However, I'd always intended to be my own boss, and I was very fortunate to have some preparation for it in youth as my parents had been self-employed my entire life. Like other kids, I read comic books and filched my father's *Playboys*, but I was also reading *Think and Grow Rich*, listening to Earl Nightingale tapes, working in the business, riding with my grandmother on job deliveries to clients, and writing up my list of life goals. This is not a mandatory prerequisite to later success. I know plenty of wildly successful entrepreneurs who came from much less helpful backgrounds. But I did have the edge of clear intent from the start of my adult life and little time to acquire the bad habits of thought and behavior that most longtime employees of other people have to shed when switching to entrepreneurship.

I think that to succeed you must not only make a firm and committed decision to do just that but you must also decide to quickly, even eagerly, give up long-held attitudes and behaviors that fit fine in your previous environment but do not work well in entrepreneurial life. Although I don't swim, I imagine it'd be tough to swim across a good-sized lake while clinging to a boat anchor. Letting go of anchors from your former life as you dive into entrepreneurial waters is essential.

Why Trying Doesn't Work

Some people think and talk in terms of "trying" a business or "trying" out the entrepreneurial experience. Before achieving major success in business myself, I went through considerable agony, corporate and personal bankruptcy, stress, embarrassment, humiliation, and near-starvation. If I'd been just "trying," just taking a test-drive, I'd have quit. And make no mistake about it; my experience is the norm among ultimately successful entrepreneurs.

Rich DeVos plunked down millions to buy the rights to an NBA franchise, the Orlando Magic, apparently to indulge himself. Every year for as long as I can recall, Rich and his lifelong partner Jay VanAndel have appeared on the annual *Forbes* magazine list of the 400 richest men in America. Certainly many envy DeVos as the wealthy, powerful co-founder of Amway Corporation, who is able to buy a basketball team!

But I wonder how many envied Rich and Jay when they were barely surviving in business, bottling a liquid cleanser in a decrepit gas station, delivering drums of the gunk cross-country to their few distributors in their own pickup truck, being laughed at by friends and family.

My student, client, and friend Jeff Paul most certainly thought about quitting and giving up on his vision of a successful mail-order business when he was awash in credit card debt, living with his family in his sister-in-law's basement. But he wasn't trying out the idea. He was committed and determined. He is wealthy today not because he tried, but because he *did*.

Another client of mine, who asked not to be named in this story, started in business immediately after going through a bankruptcy and was struggling. His wife even got their minister to try convincing him to "stop the foolishness, stop punishing his family and get a job." His business today makes millions of dollars a year. Fortunately for everybody concerned, including the doubting wife and skeptical minister, my client wasn't just trying out an idea.

My occasional client and one of my best friends, Lee Milteer, is universally respected and sometimes envied by her colleagues. Her career as a professional speaker and coach is thriving. As a speaker, she routinely commands $5,000.00 to $7,000.00 per speech. But when I met Lee, her speaking career was floundering, she was over $35,000.00 in the hole, pawning jewelry to print brochures, and taking more calls from bill collectors than from clients. In the asset column of her balance sheet, she had little more than a burning desire and determination to succeed in this unusual business.

Although Lee has developed into a great speaker, I frankly know a number of others, more naturally gifted, more professionally talented, and more skilled than she is who failed in their attempts at the business. They "tried" it, couldn't make it work, and went back to work in other jobs. Lee's good-humored determination made all the difference in the world.

Making and Keeping Faith with Your Commitments

Succeeding as an entrepreneur requires decision and determination—total, unwavering commitment. To keep faith with this commitment, you have to develop and embrace attitudes, habits, and behaviors that are markedly different from most of the people you've known. You have to cut down on time spent with people who are not supportive of your entrepreneurial ambitions. Time spent hanging around fearful people, doubtful people, skeptical people can impair your ability to succeed.

You mean I have to change my friends?

Probably. And the books you read. And the television programs you watch. And a whole lot more. We cannot help being and becoming a product of the ideas we associate with most—of the books and magazines we read, the tapes we listen to, the TV we watch, and the people we spend time with.

As thick-skinned as I believe I am and as much of an independent thinker as I pride myself in being, I admit that my performance and determination vary in relationship to what I'm reading, what I'm listening to, and who I'm hanging around with. Earl Nightingale brilliantly summarized all this, "We become what we think about most." If you are going to become an exceptionally successful entrepreneur, that is what you must think about most.

Another way to look at this is in terms of passion. The most successful entrepreneurs I know are passionately involved with entrepreneurship in general and their businesses in particular. They're in love with being entrepreneurs, excited about their products or services, "on fire" with enthusiasm—and that passion gives them superhuman powers.

This is one very good argument for belonging to entrepreneur groups, coaching programs, and peer advisory groups: you need regular contact and chances to share ideas and information with like-minded entrepreneurs who validate, support, and encourage you. My friend Joe Mancuso, a top expert in family business issues, presides over the national network of CEO (Chief Executive Officer) Clubs, which meet in dozens of cities and bring owners and presidents of midsized companies together. There's also YPO, Young Presidents Organization; YEO, Young Entrepreneurs Organization; Dan Sullivan's Strategic Coach groups; and, in many industries, specialized peer advisory groups, such as the one run by my client and friend Joe Polish in the carpet cleaning industry or Ron Ipach's group for auto repair shop owners. My own Kennedy Inner Circle Gold/VIP mastermind groups, limited to 18 members per group, meet three times a year and have tele-coaching sessions other months. In these groups, entrepreneurs from diverse businesses—dentists, lawyers, painting company owners, manufacturers, genealogists, pest control company owners and so on—come together to coach each other, and the results are amazing. I encourage every entrepreneur to seek out a coaching program or a mastermind group to participate in. Or, if you can't find one, start one.

You can greatly accelerate your entrepreneurial success and decrease your isolation-related stress by associating with other progressive entrepreneurs.

You cannot immunize yourself against the influences of the ideas of the people you associate with. There is no vaccination to protect you from negative, antibusiness thinking. For this reason, you must immerse yourself in associations that are in harmony with your goals and aspirations.

This doesn't mean you must socialize only with other entrepreneurs. I have friends who are college professors, corporate executives, actors, athletes, office workers, and so on, but I choose them carefully. They do not have negative attitudes about businesspeople; they do have interesting ambitions within their careers or are tied to other outside interests that are stimulating.

Unfortunately, you are going to discover that the majority of people, nonentrepreneurs, have a number of set-in-cement biases and frustrations with you, the entrepreneur. Let's talk about some of the big ones you'll run up against.

Accusation: You're a Workaholic

Most entrepreneurs I know experience great conflicts between their commitment to business and other aspects of their lives:

marriage, family, civic activities, and so on. Having two failed marriages in my background, I'm hypersensitive to this conflict, and I'm always working on ways to handle it more effectively. The fact—and it is fact—that the line between "work" and "play" is thoroughly blurred for the true entrepreneur and the corollary fact that the entrepreneur's business life is often, frankly, bluntly, more important to him than his personal and social life are a huge source of befuddlement, annoyance, and tension for those around him.

It's convenient and easy for others to label the determined, passionate entrepreneur as a workaholic—a diseased, neurotic addict guilty of neglecting nonwork responsibilities, of not loving his or her spouse or family, of being a self-absorbed ass. It's convenient and easy, but overly simplistic and certainly not very helpful.

In reality, the constantly working entrepreneur may be saner and happier than the critics. Most people detest their jobs, yet they continue going to them day after day, month after month, year after year. They spend the lion's share of their lives doing things they find boring and unfulfilling, but lack the guts to do anything about it. They live for the weekend. By contrast, entrepreneurs manage to stay involved in work so enjoyable and fulfilling that they no longer think of it as work.

The lovers, friends, parents, and others who throw around the workaholic label secretly resent their own "stuckedness" and try to make themselves feel better by attacking you, by making you feel guilty.

We could dismiss the critics as jealous, resentful, and unreasonable just as easily as they label us as workaholics. However, no one wants to go through life married only to a business. We need mates, family, and close friends. And they won't all be involved in our businesses or even in business. We don't get to choose our families and, besides, diversity in social life is healthy and necessary. So, better understanding of ourselves and others, recognition of the special problem we present to others, and creative efforts at preserving balances are all very important.

The problem also, ironically, reveals the greatest of all secrets to entrepreneurial success.

One study done some years back by *Venture* magazine and *Control Data* surveyed and analyzed more than 700 entrepreneurs, all of whom had operated their own businesses for at least four years and had annual incomes of at least $90,000.00. The researchers found that "the lines between work and play are obscured for most successful entrepreneurs." Not a surprising result. No survey needed. If you observe any successful entrepreneur, you'll find, for them, work is play.

One of the ultimate object lessons in this is Richard Branson, founder of Virgin Airlines and all the other Virgin companies and brands. He told *Fortune* magazine: "I don't think of work as work and play as play. It's all living."

Dan Kennedy's
Eternal Truth #2

If it's work, it won't
make you rich.

This attitude is so foreign to someone raised and conditioned in or living the 9-to-5, thank-God-it's-Friday reality, you could borrow the book title and say entrepreneurs are from Mars, others from Venus.

Typical entrepreneurs are constantly initiating new projects, even new businesses, to justify the long day, to keep the game alive. They are not just motivated by desirable end results; they're equally motivated by the enjoyment and thrill they derive from the whole process of business. They love the "action." If this is workaholism, I'm guilty.

But, also, thanks to divorces, aging, long conversations with wiser people, and many other factors, I'm developing an appreciation for balancing that passion with other passions, so that I'm less guilty. And I've discovered a very odd secret. A difficult one for everybody raised on "work ethic" like me, but here it is: outworking everybody else on the planet is NOT the best path to success as an entrepreneur. As a matter of fact, figuring out how to work less is far more useful. Over the past ten years, I've been systematically shedding businesses and responsibilities, cutting back on involvements, each year warning my CPA and tax advisor to anticipate a significant drop in my earnings. But the opposite has occurred.

My Platinum Inner Circle Member and client Ron LeGrand has this saying:

The Less I Do, The More I Make

Ron is a hugely successful real estate investor and entrepreneur, juggling literally hundreds of projects.

You have to be very careful about how you interpret this particular adage. You can't take it literally, cut your work hours in half, sleep in a hammock, and expect your income to leap up. But there are many applications of this idea that work brilliantly. For example, the less you do that others could do—the more you do that only you can do—the more you make. Or, the less you do that feels too much like uninteresting, unfulfilling work and the more you do that feels like fun, the more you make.

Succeeding in business is a real magic trick. Succeeding in business and having a balanced life is an even greater, more challenging, more worthwhile trick. Because anything and everything is possible for the determined person, why not set your sights on the very best?

Some entrepreneurs manage to involve those close to them in their work-absorbed behavior. Tom Monaghan, the founder of Domino's Pizza, gratefully tells of his wife's patience when he would always choose a pizza joint to check out whenever they were traveling or on vacation. Some fortunate couples share the same entrepreneurial passion and have that work for them.

But what if you're making the big transition from employee to entrepreneur with a spouse who is happy with your old behavior? Or what if you're involved with someone who cannot survive in a relationship dominated by your entrepreneurial passion?

Some of these relationships end. If yours is to survive, you need to be very aware of the strain that your new entrepreneurial personality, passion, and lifestyle is going to create and take proactive, preventive steps to make up for it. Then hope for the best, but be prepared for the worst.

Perception: You're a Wild-Eyed Risk Taker, a Riverboat Gambler. Have You Lost Your Mind?

One of the things that frightens many people and their loved ones about choosing the entrepreneurial lifestyle is the risk. It's interesting that our society chooses the cautious "be careful" as a means of saying goodbye to a friend. We don't say "be successful" or "be happy;" we say, "be careful."

The true entrepreneur prefers to be adventurous and "fail forward" all the time. Running a business *is* a risk, but it needn't be foolhardy. I rarely make a decision without considering everything from the best-case scenario to the worst-case scenario. I try to expect the best and insure against the worst.

Most people see things as black or white: someone is either the meek and mild Clark Kent or the strong and daring Superman. They try to see themselves instantly turning from Kent to Superman and have understandable difficulty conceiving and believing in such a miraculous transition.

Such dramatic overnight makeovers rarely occur. People grow into and with their new roles. You *can* start from where you are and grow to where you want to be. Anxiety about the risks inherent in business is natural. But the real objective of the entrepreneur is to *manage* risk, not to *take* risk.

Everybody manages risk every day. For example, statistics indicate that the risk of having a home fire during a lifetime is very high. Some people sensibly manage this risk by installing smoke and heat detectors, checking the batteries periodically, keeping an escape ladder in the hall closet, devising and rehearsing an escape plan with the kids, having surge protectors for major appliances, and so on. This is thorough risk management.

Other people just install a smoke detector and forget about it. They are managing the risk to a lesser degree.

Still others do nothing at all. They *take* the risk.

The successful entrepreneur deals with carefully calculated, measured risk. He demands accurate, complete information from

As an aside, let me give you an important observation about how entrepreneurs get into trouble more often than not: they fail to gather readily available information before making decisions and commitments. As a consultant, I can usually stump most clients with just three questions about the history of their planned business ventures. Very few people bother to do any homework. They merely have an idea and act on it, like a child grabbing candy from a grocery store shelf on impulse.

I'm unceasingly amazed at the people who start businesses without even studying the history of the industry they've chosen to enter. Far too many entrepreneurs fritter away far too much time needlessly inventing and experimenting when they could be implementing because they don't know much about anything that happened before yesterday!

Information gathering is a very important task for the entrepreneur. I realize it sounds dull, feels slow, but nevertheless, the quality of information you amass and consider will have a great deal of impact on the outcome of your decisions. At www.nobsbooks.com/free, I've posted a *Guide to Research Sources for Entrepreneurs*, which you can download free of charge. It's on the Internet so we can periodically update it.

associates and advisors and welcomes input and ideas from credible sources. But he also knows when to stop and avoid the paralysis of never-ending analysis.

There's a balance between too little and too much caution. In J. R. R. Tolkien's book *The Hobbit*, the wizard Gandalf offers Bilbo Baggins an opportunity to go on a great adventure with the potential of acquiring great riches at the end. Bilbo responds with his perspective on adventures: "Nasty disturbing uncomfortable things! Make you late for dinner."

Somewhere between the extremes of unbridled risk and Bilbo's total aversion to adventure, you will find your balance as an entrepreneur. As you gradually develop that sense of balance as a risk manager and decision maker, you'll find that you can function without much stress or anxiety.

Big Lie: The Price of Entrepreneurial Success Is Just Too Much to Pay

For some, that's a true statement, but for others, it's a big lie. There are some people who really will be happier and more productive in nonentrepreneurial roles. But there's also great misunderstanding about the price of success.

Every lifestyle, every choice has its price. The person who follows the old model of staying in a good job with a good company for 40 years may pay the price in boredom, frustration, and quiet desperation of unfulfilled, untested potential.

Today, people who try to stay with that model often pay an even higher price when a merger, acquisition, downsizing, bankruptcy, or even disappearance of an entire industry put long-time employees out on the street. They must tackle a dynamic, tough job market with outdated skills and face the future without the financial security they believed was guaranteed to them for their loyalty and longevity. Entrusting your success to others in corporate bureaucracies is increasingly risky business.

Then there are the legions of "gray people." I don't mean aging; I mean pallid, pasty, near-dead looking. Every morning they march off to a job they have no interest in doing well and derive nothing from but an unsatisfactory paycheck. Every night they come home bored and boring. The price they pay is huge, but it is a slow, almost invisible dying. If you look close, though, you can see it in their eyes.

Yes, entrepreneurial life exacts a high price—often in ways everyone around you dislikes intensely. As chief cook and bottle washer, you've got nobody to call in sick to. While the employee leaves at 5:00 P.M. whether work is done or not, you can't. If there's a deadline looming, you must meet it, even if that means skipping dinner, your kid's school recital, sleep.

In one interview, the daughter of Dave Thomas, founder and developer of the Wendy's fast food chain, was asked if her father came to her school events. She said she doubted if he even knew where her school was! Yes, the entrepreneur's family pays a price too.

However, I know plenty of fathers who are physically home every night and every weekend but mentally and emotionally elsewhere. Or who constantly concoct excuses to get away from their families—like golf, a game that clearly would never have been invented if marriage hadn't been invented first.

The reality is this: you don't get to choose a life without a price. There are options, but each has a different price.

There are two sides to the price of entrepreneurship. As an example, consider illness or death in the family. My father was ill in his later years, and there was some real risk he might be suddenly rushed to the hospital and die without much warning. I knew, if I was en route to a speaking engagement or in a distant city honoring a speaking commitment, I would not be able to "stiff" the seminar promoter. My father would wait, and I would honor my contractual commitment. That never happened. When the time came and he was rushed to the hospital, I was able to drop what I was doing, buy a ticket without blinking, and fly across country for a good, lengthy, final visit. I also supported him financially, entirely, for more than ten years.

The person in a "normal job" gets family leave. The entrepreneur does not. The employee has one boss, the entrepreneur many. In many ways, the employee has it easier in doing the things in family life generally regarded by most people as correct and appropriate, but it is quite often the "odd man out" entrepreneur in the family everyone else turns to, to get out the checkbook and pay the bills the others can't. His willingness to pay the price for entrepreneurial success is what makes it possible for him to pay the tab in a family crisis or tragedy.

The upshot is that you the entrepreneur must be prepared for, and rather thick-skinned toward, the criticism of the nonentrepreneurs in your life about the price they perceive you pay for your success.

The Decision of Autonomy

When you depend on others, you collect and store up excuses for failure like Harry does. Harry doesn't like his too-small, in-disrepair house. He doesn't like his five-year-old, mechanically ailing car. He doesn't like the pile of bills in the kitchen drawer. He hates his job. He doesn't respect his boss. But wait, the one thing he does have going for him is a book of excuses. He opens it up and sighs with relief: *This sorry state of affairs isn't my fault. My mother liked my brother more and that gave me an inferiority complex. We grew up on the wrong side of the tracks. My family couldn't afford to send me to college.* And on and on and on.

This is called burying yourself in B.S. If you really want to be a success in business, you need to be *emotionally* independent before you can ever become *financially* independent.

To succeed as an entrepreneur, you must set aside your neediness for acceptance from others. Immunity to criticism is a "secret" shared by *all* the highly successful entrepreneurs that I know.

To succeed as an entrepreneur, you have to set aside your "Book of Excuses" once and for all. Making money as an entrepreneur and making excuses are mutually exclusive, wholly incompatible.

The sooner you arrive at accepting 100% responsibility for everything, the more successful you'll be. Go take a look in the mirror. There's the man or woman—the *only* man or woman—who can make you happy, thin, rich, famous, or whatever it is that you aspire to. Dr. Phil can't *make* you thin, McDonald's doesn't *make* you fat.

The power you need and can have as an entrepreneur comes from eschewing all excuses never blaming the economy, the government, the competition, the timing, your parents, your school, or anything or anyone else for anything. Ultimate power comes from accepting total responsibility. When you believe as I do that circumstances control other people but not me, then circumstances won't control you either.

A very common occurrence in America in recent years has been Wal-Mart coming into a town and lots of little mom-'n-pop

I feel fortunate to have discovered a lot about this very early in life.

If I ever got an allowance, it stopped when I was still a little kid. I don't remember it. I do remember earning my spending money very early on. I picked strawberries and packaged tomatoes at the greenhouses behind our community, cleaned stalls at a nearby stable, and washed and waxed cars. I soon figured out that selling was easier than manual labor, so I spent my teen years selling. I sold business printing and advertising specialties, Stuart McGuire shoes, and a new plasticized, reusable carbon paper; and I became involved in a multilevel marketing company.

In my early experiences in direct and multilevel sales, I quickly found out that most of my distributors (even though they were 5 to 25 years older and more "mature" than I was) could not be relied on even to have the appropriate literature, samples, and other materials with them at presentations! If I wanted prospects handled properly, I had to take steps to make up for the others' lack of organization, discipline, and reliability; I had to have extra supplies on hand. This sales experience taught me the importance of self-reliance and the futility of relying on others.

businesses rolling over and dying. Their owners blame Wal-Mart. There have been protest marches. Books written. Much handwringing about behemoth Wal-Mart destroying small businesses left and right. All utter and total B.S. And here's the proof: there are small businesses who have thrived when Wal-Mart came to their towns. Why? Because they didn't embrace the

---

My Platinum Member and publisher of my *No B.S. Marketing Letter*, Bill Glazer, is case in point. In downtown Baltimore there once were 14 competing menswear stores, each independently owned. As giant national chains entered the market, 13 of those stores closed. The last store standing, one of two thriving stores owned by Bill, has most recently ably withstood heavy, direct competition from the giant discounter, Mens Wearhouse. In fact, his stores have enjoyed double-digit annual growth while his industry has been flat, and they generate per square foot profits 250 percent higher than the industry average. How can this be?

For one thing, Bill is an ingenious, aggressive marketer. But possibly of greater significance is his *attitude* about the competition, his conviction that he can always reposition his own business and outmaneuver the big behemoths.

---

excuse for failure. They re-engineered their businesses to do what the giant won't, to compete in a different way.

Entrepreneurial success requires a very, very strong sense of autonomy. The definition from my dictionary of *autonomy* is *self-governing*. Simple. Good. It says a lot.

For example, it says you make your own rules. You feel free to ignore or violate or at the very least, challenge and test all established norms of your industry. To ignore competitive pricing and, instead, devise a marketing system that has you selling in a competitive vacuum—which happens to be my "specialty" as a marketing strategist and consultant. You decide to do business on your terms, to fit your preferences, which I talk a lot about in this book's companion volume, *No B.S. Time Management.*

It also means you govern your own thoughts and emotions and do not let others dictate how you should think or what you should believe.

The truly legendary mega-entrepreneurs I admire and have studied exhaustively were or are intensely self-governing.

Walt Disney, for example, violated the established, universal, ironclad amusement park industry "rule" of multiple entrances and exits. Against all expert advice, he designed Disneyland with but one entrance and egress. Although he did not do so for purely mercenary reasons, it's impossible to estimate the enormous volume of souvenir merchandise sales that occur precisely because everyone must "walk the plank" past the stores and merchandise carts to get out of the park.

Disney resisted profit-based temptation and the urging of his own executives and bankers, stubbornly refusing to permit the sale of any alcoholic beverages on the park's grounds, instead preserving the wholesome family atmosphere that is at the very core of the Disney appeal.

Walt was one of the great "Unreasonable Men"—a description that fits most terrific entrepreneurs. My friend and speaking colleague, Mike Vance, who worked closely with Walt for many years, tells the true story of Walt being told by a waitress that "something didn't seem right" about the new Pirates of the Caribbean restaurant next to the ride. Disney then abruptly shut the entire thing down, shooed away all but a few of the customers, sacrificed revenue and created havoc, then conducted an impromptu focus group to get to the bottom of what "didn't seem right." It turned out to be the absence of fireflies, which Walt demanded be fixed by importing fireflies. Time and time again, Walt drove his bean-counter brother crazy, demanding things be done—often expensive and difficult things—to achieve the exceptional authenticity the parks are famous for.

Walt put Disneyland in a location no one thought could possibly work.

The cliché "he walks to the beat of his own drum" applied magnificently to Walt. As it does to Trump.

Donald Trump is so famous he needs only one name, Trump. Like Cher. Most established experts in commercial real estate development avoid branding their properties with their name, as traditional industry belief has been that doing so made it difficult to attract top tenants or to later sell the property. Trump has been sharply criticized and ridiculed for slapping his own name on every building he develops. However, he says that as soon as the Trump name goes up on one, its value pops up by 10% to 15%.

Men like these *are* self-governing. They break rules, rewrite rules with impunity, daring, and, often, arrogance.

Being self-governing is, in a way, a state of mind acted out through entrepreneurship.

I have a client, Stephen Snyder, author of the bestselling book *Credit after Bankruptcy*, who typifies or demonstrates the profound need for emotional autonomy.

Snyder painfully recovered from his own bankruptcy by wrestling with predatory lenders and gradually discovering how to manage credit scores, credit reports, and credit bureaus in order to buy a car or a home and get credit cards at low interest rates. He then determined there was a business opportunity in teaching his secrets to other recently bankrupt individuals. His wife loathed the risks of entrepreneurship, doubted the viability of his ideas, and argued relentlessly against his fledgling business venture. Virtually any and every business expert asked for advice reacted the same way: how nutty can you be to try and develop an entire business dealing only with *bankrupt* people?

Today, Stephen Snyder's company puts on more than 100 seminars a year throughout the United States, with 400 to 700 recently bankrupt individuals attending each one. The firm is responsible for bestselling books for this target market and even publishes a magazine exclusively for the recently bankrupt. His firm also organizes and provides home buying, mortgage, automobile buying and financing, and other credit-oriented services; individual coaching via telephone and the Internet; and even legal services for the recently bankrupt. His company is a huge success.

As of this writing, I am working with Stephen to produce and air his first TV infomercial. It may or may not succeed; it is an unproven category for the infomercial medium. But, as a good entrepreneur would tell you, nothing ventured, nothing gained!

Mental Toughness Required

The autonomy you develop will stand you in good stead when your business hits some of the rough roads. Which it will.

One sad truth about business is that you never finish with the same people you start with. Partners, friends, key employees, and others will fall by the wayside for one reason or another as you go along. You will outgrow some. Others will become jealous and resentful of you. I can assure you that, at some point, you will have to make a decision that will be very unpopular with everybody around you. Then you will ultimately decide that the only indispensable person in your business is you.

Recently, a Member of one of my coaching groups, a top DUI and criminal trial attorney in a major southwestern city, came to grips with his need to get rid of a soured employee. He procrastinated for more than a year, tolerating her bad attitude, sabotage of his authority with other employees, and almost constant criticism of his ideas. He argued with me that she was indispensable. She'd been with him for 13 years, knew his business inside and out. She managed the office, interacted with clients, even accompanied him to court. He had erred in letting this one person become so apparently indispensable, but it ultimately turned out she wasn't quite as indispensable as she or he thought. In the two months immediately following her departure, the number of new cases increased, revenues increased, other employees stepped up to the plate.

I once had to end a five-year relationship with a business partner who had been my closest, best friend. At another time, an 11-year working relationship with a lawyer who had become a friend and who had gone through many battles with me also had to be ended. I've had to fire long-time employees I personally liked. And I've had to put my foot down, have a confrontation, and endure temporary anger and tension in the work environment.

But, ultimately, business cannot be run by committee or consensus. You're it.

Being *it* is not always fun. But always necessary.

Hey, That's Not Fair!

A lot of people respond to their various handicaps, problems, and disappointments with the complaint, "It's just not fair." And it sure isn't. For starters, we don't get to pick our parents. There's a flaw in the system right there! Next, most of us aren't movie-star gorgeous. But all this pales in comparison to the biggest injustice and mystery of all, the frequency with which bad things happen to good people.

A young man, Donald R., an honor student, considerate, courteous, and athletically talented, had an accident on the high school trampoline, landed on his back across the frame, and wound up paralyzed in both legs and in both arms for life. He had to make a choice. He could have retreated into isolation, devoted his life to self-pity and bitterness, and lived as a helpless invalid. Instead, Donald R. learned to focus the entire force of his personality through his voice so he could use the telephone, the only tool that lets him travel anywhere in the world while in a wheelchair, to become an enormously successful businessman.

Dialing with a pencil clenched in his teeth, he became one of the most proficient telemarketers in his chosen industry. He supported himself with dignity. He made the money to have a beautiful home custom built with every imaginable convenience and gadget to help him function as if he weren't handicapped. He became an inspiration to others in his field and to other handicapped people. He was influential in his community, generous to good causes, completely productive, and proud. He enjoyed an active social life and a happy marriage.

There is no argument that Donald got dealt a lousy hand. Bad things *do* happen to good people, and sometimes wc have little or no control over such things. However, we *can* control our reactions to the cards we are dealt. After Donald had his accident, he dumped a few cards, drew a few new cards, and changed his hand by choice.

I knew Donald R. personally many years ago, when I was in direct sales. More recently, I've appeared on a number of seminar-events where Christopher Reeve was another of the speakers. Imagine suddenly being dealt his hand. Going from a physically imposing, athletic, dynamic actor known to many as "Superman," to someone completely immobilized, wheelchair captive, totally dependent. He has still chosen to pursue a multifaceted career as a professional speaker, author, actor, and producer, even though the very act of getting out of bed is a Herculean project. He is even forcing the medical establishment to very reluctantly reconsider its position that certain spinal cord injuries are irreversible.

That's why there are always people who pull themselves out of the worst ghettos in America to become successful, prominent businesspeople, top athletes, and good family men and women. Oprah Winfrey is just one example of someone who proves this point. She emerged from the horror of child abuse to become the top female talk show host in America, a talented actress, and a savvy entrepreneur.

We choose our reactions. We decide what happens next. Complaining, whining, and proclaiming the unfairness of the situation does nothing to improve it.

I'm sort of an unjustified success. I'm woefully unqualified for just about everything I do.

As I recall, I got a C in high school speech class and probably deserved worse. I had a rather severe stuttering problem three different speech therapists failed to cure. If you had seen me stuttering and stammering as a kid, you wouldn't have wagered a nickel on my future as a professional speaker. Incredibly, I rose to success and prominence, including nine consecutive years on the biggest, most-envied-by-other-speakers seminar tour in America. The tour included dozens of cities each year with audiences as large as 35,000; I appeared with former U.S. presidents, world leaders, Hollywood celebrities, famous athletes, and other top speakers. By any reasonable appraisal, I didn't belong there. I chose to be there.

The fact that I earn a large income as a writer would be a heart attack-sized surprise to my English and journalism teachers. In total, I've had nine books published. My first business book, *The Ultimate Sales Letter,* has become something of a "bible" for advertising copywriters and has been continuously available in bookstores since 1991. That kind of longevity is rare. My books have been translated into five languages and published in 20 countries.

Over the years I've talked to a lot of people *thinking about* writing a book. Many hold back because they feel they aren't qualified. That's a double whammy—a self-image deficiency and an inaccurate appraisal of the way the marketplace works. Others have written books but not done what is necessary to market them. Generally, everybody's waiting for somebody else to discover them, certify them, anoint them, invest in them, instead of deciding to make happen what they want to happen.

I'm also responsible for the sale of tens of millions of dollars of merchandise each year through the advertising that I create, but I have no formal training in that field.

I could go on with other resume items, all the result of decision, not of qualification.

Personally, I prefer being an unjustified success rather than a justified failure.

One corner of my office is graced by a huge, stuffed Yogi Bear. He's there to remind me of his favorite saying: "I'm smarter than the average bear." That's me: smarter than the average bear. I'm not necessarily better educated, or better qualified, or better capitalized, or better connected. But I'm "street-smarter." Go ahead, I say, run your best at me. I'll keep figuring out new ways to win faster than anybody else can manufacture new obstacles! *That* is the attitude of the entrepreneur who makes it big.

Some cynic once said, "There is no justice. Only power." As an entrepreneur, you have tremendous opportunity to acquire the power of control over all aspects of your life. I'm not talking about the kind of power you lord over everybody—bullying power, brute power. I mean the power to arrange your life as you desire it to be, to associate with people you really enjoy and benefit from being with, to earn an income truly commensurate with your contributions, to live where you most want to live, and to travel or stay home. Your finances are not controlled by some corporate bureaucracy or the whim of a boss. You write your own paycheck.

I have, for example, arranged my business affairs so that I can take many minivacations, linked to business travel, as well as extended vacations without worry. I can work at home and let my office run itself. I never have to sit in rush-hour traffic. I get to pick and choose clients and projects.

You get power by deciding to have power.

CHAPTER 2

The Real Entrepreneurial Experience: A No B.S. Report from the Front Lines

I'm only an average man, but, by George, I work harder at it than the average man.

—THEODORE ROOSEVELT

The entrepreneur suffers more bureaucratic foolishness than you can possibly imagine until you deal with it first-hand. As an entrepreneur, you are drafted into service without compensation as a bookkeeper and tax collector for at least three different governments (federal, state, city) and for at least a dozen different taxes, some dealt with twice monthly, some monthly, some quarterly, and some annually. There is nothing that politicians and bureaucrats understand less or that costs and frustrates entrepreneurs more than this enslavement to government.

Some years ago, I had one friend, an owner of a small retail business, who got so angry over all this that one day, when his mail was filled with more letters from government agencies than anything else, he had a heart attack, tax notice clutched in hand.

Former senator and presidential candidate George McGovern bought a bed-and-breakfast as a retirement adventure. Subsequently, in an article he wrote for *Inc.* magazine, he confessed that he was overwhelmed with the nonsensical, outrageous government interference in his business. He said, had he understood this when in the U.S. Senate, he'd have voted very differently on a large number of issues and laws. McGovern subsequently filed bankruptcy and publicly blamed much of it on the burdens government layered on his business. He even noted, "A critical promotional campaign never got off the ground because my manager was forced to concentrate for days at a time on needlessly complicated tax forms for both the IRS and the state of Connecticut."

This points out the fatal flaw of a noncitizen government, one taken over by professional politicians lacking real world experience.

For entertainment, take a look at this "legal document" (Figure 2.1) that I created and published in my *No B.S. Marketing Letter.* Feel free to copy it and share it with any other business

> If you've read Ayn Rand, as most entrepreneurs have and all entrepreneurs should, you can certainly see the events of her visionary novel *Atlas Shrugged* marching toward us with frightening and depressing speed and apparent inevitability.

owner you think might enjoy it. It speaks to the current litigious and regulatory-intensive environment in which we operate.

Pride Is Sometimes the Only Pay

Government interference and idiocy, tax upon tax, regulation upon regulation, is only one of the many severely annoying, emotionally challenging distractions from productivity that the entrepreneur confronts hour by hour, day by day. There are employee problems, vendor problems, financing problems, customer problems, and competitor problems. On top of all that, there are the times when nothing's going right and red ink is flowing all over the checkbook like blood.

Almost every legendary entrepreneur is severely tested at one time or another, one way or another.

When I interviewed Tom Monaghan of Domino's Pizza years ago, he talked about going from "entrepreneurial wiz kid" to "village idiot" overnight. Trump once nearly went broke. Bill Gates has been mired in federal antitrust litigation for years.

I think one of the secrets to success is that, no matter what, you have to crawl out from under, set aside, and ignore all the bureaucratic B.S., the million little irritations and problems, even the crises, in order to keep the process of getting, serving, and satisfying customers as your number-one priority. This is easier said than done. There's so much of the *other* that entrepreneurs and their typically small, overworked staffs can too easily fall into the trap of viewing the customer as an interruption and obstacle to getting the necessary work done.

Sometimes, when the problems are overwhelming, pride is the only immediate reward. You'll be hard pressed, for example, to find

A while ago, Ron LeGrand, one of my long-time clients and Platinum Inner Circle Members, had, through his personal efforts as a top author, speaker, and consultant on residential real estate investment, built up a $20 million-plus a year company. But through a sequence of misjudgments, others' greed, partner disputes, and attempts to go public, he actually lost control not only of his own company but also of all the copyrights to his own books and courses, even to his own students' testimonials. In December 2002, he was unceremoniously escorted by security guards out of his own building. A court action was filed by his adversaries attempting to prohibit him even from speaking for fees on his own expertise.

While many would panic or rail against the injustice or roll up in a ball and die, Ron is a true entrepreneur. He methodically went to work on the problems, but he also instantly went to work creating an entirely new business, new products, new opportunities. He operated simultaneously on multiple tracks, all aimed at the same chief objectives. In only a few months, he had settled the dispute, re-acquired all his products and publishing rights, and developed a new, fast-growing, much more profitable company.

an entrepreneur who hasn't had the experience of meeting the payroll by the skin of his teeth, having nothing left over to take home to the family, having to tell the kids they can't afford this or that, taking calls at home from personal bill collectors, and then lying awake at night, staring at the ceiling, wondering if, at next paycheck time, it will be any different. But pride can keep you going.

There is the axiom: it is difficult to remember your objective of draining the swamp when you are up to your ass in alligators. But that is exactly what is required of the entrepreneur.

Even when I was at the helm of an ill-advisedly acquired, deeply troubled, money-hemorrhaging, chaos-and-crisis-riddled corporation, I pulled myself out of the alligator-fighting for at least one hour every day to refocus on the objectives, to get something done that was positive and productive and goal directed.

Take a Trip Down Lonely Street

Whether you're winning or losing at the moment, the isolation of the entrepreneurial experience is surprising and dangerous. This was expressed well in an article in *Entrepreneur* magazine (July 1990) by Beverly Bernstein, who left a job with Mattel Toys to start her own consulting business. After two years, her business was booming, and she was earning twice her old salary, but she missed the camaraderie of the corporate workplace. "When you start your own business, you don't have the same collegial relationships as when you work inside a company," Beverly explained. "I missed the laughter and the interchange of ideas. I missed the energy. And I miss them."

The entrepreneurs in my coaching groups talk about the isolation they often feel. They lament having no one of like mind and common understanding to brag to about their victories or to discuss their problems. Participation in my coaching groups is a partial antidote for them. But the isolation of the entrepreneur is real.

As an employee, many decisions are made for you, many more are arrived at through consensus. A social environment with friendship is provided. And, at the end of the day, if there's work yet undone, in most cases, you go home, shrug it off on the way, and pretty much ignore it. All that changes dramatically when you own the business.

I doubt there's anything as totally absorbing as the entrepreneurial experience. Pro athletes and their coaches certainly live their businesses, but they have off days, even off seasons, and rest periods. They get paychecks, and they don't have to worry about attendance, network viewership, merchandise sales, and budgets. The entrepreneur has to play the game *and* run the business.

It's even difficult to maintain your regular social life. People you used to enjoy getting together with suddenly seem different, their concerns and conversations trivial, their daily experiences so different from yours that there's no longer any common ground. In many cases, their attitudes are so different from yours that you can't afford to be around them.

I'm an Overnight Success—After 20 Years

It is only in the last dozen years that I've experienced substantial, consistently increasing success in my businesses. There were many years of struggle. In the darkest days, I would run around all day telling employees, associates, vendors, and investors not to worry, that I knew what I was doing, that everything would be OK. Then I would lock myself in the bathroom, look in the mirror, and call myself a liar. Not a day went by that I didn't have to convince myself to continue.

This tests the very core of your being. I am sure there are tougher tests, such as the real life-and-death tests of character faced by soldiers at war, firefighters, and police officers or those faced by people diagnosed with terminal diseases. But the tests imposed by the entrepreneurial experience must come in a close second.

Consider, for example, the speaking career part of my business. From 1991 through 2000, I was one of the featured speakers on tour with the motivational superstar Zig Ziglar and many celebrity speakers at heavily advertised all-day events, addressing tens of thousands of people in each city, in about 25 cities each year, often selling $50,000.00 to $70,000.00 or more of my books and cassettes per hour. This contributed to my being sought out and given other top speaking opportunities, helped raise my speaking fees, and made me the envy of many of my peers. As a result, more than one professional speaker has said to me, "You lucky dog."

Attributing it to luck is an insult.

I started speaking in 1977. In one year, I gave free talks, selling tickets to my own seminars, in more than 100 real estate, insurance, and other sales offices, often to groups of just three, five, or ten people. Sometimes people were inattentive or downright rude; while I spoke, they answered their phones, read their newspapers, and slurped their coffee. It didn't help that I wasn't a very good speaker.

In my first ten years of speaking, there were plenty of horror stories. Seminars where hardly anybody showed up and I lost money. Tough, tough audiences. I went on tours of five cities in five days, driving across the country to make it to each. Grinding, grueling travel. Countless motel rooms with defective air-conditioning, heat, or plumbing. I could go on. *But every business has its own version of such an obstacle course, to brutally separate the weak from the strong.*

After all, if it was too easy, everybody would do it, and it would be devalued.

Every "overnight success" knows there's no such thing.

Even with Success, There Is Failure

Because the entrepreneur is always innovating, experimenting, and pioneering, there's always failure mixed with success: the new ad, the new products, or the new service that doesn't work—or worse.

A friend of mine, Ted G., sold his company early this year for more than $6 million. He started it 10 years ago with $1,000.00. The day he strolled into the bank with the $6 million check, he felt that he was a pretty smart, successful, even heroic fellow. A month later, he put together a seminar, promoted it with a major advertising campaign, and lost about $40,000.00. The three days that he worked, teaching that seminar at a loss, he didn't feel so smart, successful, or heroic.

I know what this is like. In the past, I've gone bankrupt, personally and corporately. I've had my cars repossessed. I've gone from a new Lincoln to a 15-year-old Rent-a-Dent, paid for weekly in cash. I have had so little that if a burglar had broken into my apartment, he might have left a donation. As a result of the bankruptcies, I was criticized, reviled, and sneered at by professional peers, persecuted by my own trade association, and humiliated beyond belief. To give it all its best spin, let's summarize it as prolonged, profound financial embarrassment.

Today, I say with great gratitude, things are much, much better. But even at the height of success, there's failure. For example, one of the things I do in my direct marketing consulting business is create and produce TV infomercials—half-hour programs that sell merchandise—full-page magazine ads, or complicated direct-mail campaigns. For every successful show, there are many failures. A client may have put up $200,000.00 or even more and I may have hundreds of hours invested in a show that tests so miserably its first weekend on the air that there's nothing left to do but dig a large hole in the backyard, shove the master tapes in, say last rites, and walk away. That is not easy to do. For every wildly successful ad, there are flops. Almost every success has its foundation parked on a graveyard concealing the bones of failure.

The need to shake it off, regroup, bounce back, pick yourself up, dust yourself off, and start all over again is universal and reoccurring in the entrepreneurial experience.

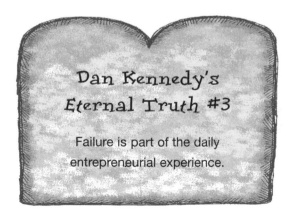

Dan Kennedy's
Eternal Truth #3

Failure is part of the daily
entrepreneurial experience.

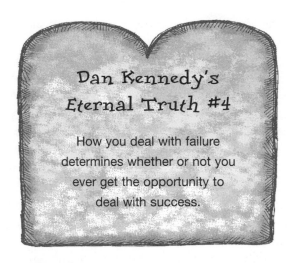

Dan Kennedy's Eternal Truth #4

How you deal with failure determines whether or not you ever get the opportunity to deal with success.

The flip side, using my speaking business as an example, is standing there on stage in front of 500, 1,000, 3,000, or 10,000 people, basking in their laughter and applause, sending them stampeding to the book and tape tables, doing more business in 60 minutes than some stores do in 60 days. In my other businesses, I glory in big orders and unsolicited letters of praise in the mail; planning a new promotion, implementing it, and seeing it work; solving a tough problem; and closing a big sale.

I don't think there's anything like the "high" of entrepreneurial success, of taking the germ of an idea and nurturing it step by step, embellishing it, developing faith in it, implementing it, making it work, and turning it into tangible, substantial rewards.

It's a kind of glory. Songwriters and musicians talk about the experience of driving down the road, fiddling with the radio, and suddenly hearing their own song come on for the first time. Most pull over to the side of the road and listen in awe to what they've wrought. We entrepreneurs get that same kind of a jolt when we see our commercial on TV, our ad in a magazine, our new store-front, our product on the store shelf. Most people never experience anything like this.

And then sometimes you make it big. Imagine being Bill Rosenberg, a high school dropout who started a little business in 1946 with $2,500.00 saved from working two or three jobs at a time, seven days a week, 12 hours a day. He has seen his little business grow into the nationwide chain, Dunkin' Donuts.

Imagine being my clients Bill Guthy and Greg Renker, who now can turn on the TV anywhere in America, anytime day or night, and land on one of their own TV infomercials. The infomercials generate hundreds of millions of dollars a year now, but this duo started humbly. Bill was in the audiocassette manu-facturing business, making product for others. Neither had any particularly relevant background or experience that would suggest their ultimate success in creating infomercials.

Imagine being my client Joe Polish, once a flat-broke, befuddled carpet cleaner nearly starved out of the business altogether, now standing on a stage in a room filled with more than 600 carpet cleaners who've traveled from all over the world to hear him explain his successful business strategies. This one group will lead to deposits of more than a million dollars in Joe's bank account in one weekend.

Imagine being another of my clients (who doesn't want to be identified), who went broke three times in a row, with three different sales companies. He now has more than 500 franchisees all over America, which he tours regularly in his own private jet.

Behind every entrepreneurial glory story, there's an investment of plenty of blood and guts.

What Ultimately Separates Entrepreneurial Winners from Losers?

There's a sign on my office door that reads, "Whatever it takes."

That is the entrepreneur's job description: holding your paychecks; loaning money to your business; working long hours; having to sell and motivate constantly; dealing with bankers, lawyers, unresponsive vendors, and other difficult folks. The list could go on. **Entrepreneurial life is the solving of the never-ending stream of problems**. People who go into business for themselves because they think they will have fewer problems than they had in their previous jobs wear down and wear out quickly.

Carter Henderson, author of the book *Winners,* observed, "To be in business is to be assaulted by relentless adversity and crisis; it comes with the territory." *The* **characteristic that tends to distinguish the winners from the losers is the relentless conversion of problems to opportunities, negatives to positives.**

Now, I don't mean classic "positive thinking" methodology. I don't believe that whistling in the dark does much to protect you from the bogeyman. If he's there, whistling won't help. For 30 years I've warned people to watch out for the misguided, militant "Positive Thinkers" who want everyone to be two of the monkeys: See No Evil and Hear No Evil.

That's how you wind up getting the World Trade Center destroyed, an anvil dropped on your head, all your money stolen, wrong diagnoses from doctors.

I recently did a day of consulting with VIP Member Chet Rowland. Chet's having a record-breaking year in his thriving, million-dollar-plus pest control business and launching his info-business in that industry. He and I discussed Murphy's Law and the necessity of having Plans B, C, and D. The militant positive thinkers would insist he is "negative." I think he's prudent, realistic, and sensible. It is a fact of life, NOT mere self-fulfilling prophecy, that most projects take longer and cost more than anticipated, most vendors screw up at the worst possible moment, almost all good employees become bad employees, etc., and the only sane response is anticipatory and proactive. I traveled extensively and learned never to depart with airline ticket in hand, without knowing when the backup flights were, in some cases having a backup reservation, and determining in advance what my Plan B would be if my flight were cancelled or the limo was not there. As a speaker, I carry my overheads with me, always have a copy of the order form with me in case FedEx loses the ones I sent, and typically carry a product sample in case the shipment is lost. For years, I carried a spare bulb for overhead projectors in my briefcase. The same behavior is warranted, universally. Oh, and incidentally, sometimes Plan B is actually superior to Plan A, which you never discover unless you do the work of creating Plan B—there's a million dollar secret for you.

There's a vast difference between earned, deserved, justifiable optimism and foolish, unwarranted, dangerous optimism. Optimism can be virtue or vice, like most things, depending on application. There are, incidentally, plenty of wildly optimistic people who are always dead broke. The single biggest optimist I have ever known was broke far more often than rich, occasionally incredibly successful but always unable to sustain it, dangerously oblivious to reality, and completely irresponsible as a business owner and organization leader, served five years in a state penitentiary, and is ending his life in a sad state of affairs—estranged from family and friends and broke. But he was the poster boy of unbridled optimism.

I'm not talking about *that* kind of thinking. Instead I'm talking about an automatic, action-oriented response that instantly dissects crisis and creates new opportunity. That "entrepreneurial reflex" makes all the difference. Will you be dead-tired or energized at the end of every day? Glum and depressed or good-humored and optimistic? Effective or paralyzed? This "reflex" makes those distinctions.

The Good News

As an entrepreneur, you do get a very special entitlement: you can depend on there being a new door to open whenever another door slams shut. In his book *Think and Grow Rich*, Napoleon Hill wrote, "In every adversity lies the seed of an equal or greater achievement."

Just about every really terrific thing that has occurred for me has come out of something really terrible. You may think I'm being a Pollyanna, but if you will dig for it, you'll find great opportunity in every adversity. In my seminars for entrepreneurs, one of the key principles I teach is:

All news is good news.

This is very difficult to accept at face value. Yet, if you closely examine your own history as I have mine, you will probably find as I have that every event that seemed negative or tragic at the time was an essential bridge to something better or to a new opportunity. Entrepreneurs understand this, their "entrepreneurial reflex" of resiliency is based on it.

So here's the resiliency question: **If X happened, what would we do?**

Sometimes the answer to that turns out to be superior to your Plan A, which is in place only because X hasn't happened.

For years I have operated my office without a receptionist, with limited and controlled "live" access hours shielding my staff from constant interruption and dramatically increasing their productivity. However that all started as "Plan B," when my mother, the receptionist, was hospitalized and then died. As an emergency, temporary measure, we went to Plan B. It quickly became clear Plan B should get a promotion to Plan A. The interesting thing is, I could have been on Plan B at least five, maybe ten years, sooner and used my mother's time and ability as an employee much more profitably. I can only wonder how much money was lost that could have been made with this system.

I got into the coaching business on a serious level to offset the income I was sacrificing from lots of speaking gigs I no longer was willing to travel to do. But couldn't I have done that three, five, seven years earlier, if I'd asked: *if I were confined to a wheelchair and couldn't travel to speak, what would I do?*

It is actually embarrassing to use 20/20 hindsight and see how many times I might have made much faster progress toward my overriding goals by much more frequently using the Plan B question. I suppose it's inspirational, and a wonderful testament to the free enterprise system, that as big an idiot as I can do as well as I have. That's the drawback to writing up information like this; you wind up rubbing your own nose in your idiocy. Not even a dog'll do that. Anyway, here's an incredibly provocative exercise: (1) make a list of as many individual things you do by rote, the person you rely on, the business methods you use, etc., and (2) ask the Plan B question regarding every single one of them. (3) Repeat same exercise at least once a year.

FIGURE 2.1: Legal Document

IMPORTANT LEGAL NOTICE

You are about to consume food substances in this restaurant that contain calories, fat, sugar, salt, carbohydrates, artificial flavors, preservatives, and other ingredients which may be, in some way, harmful to your health. Consuming inordinately large quantities of these food substances in this establishment or elsewhere or in combination thereof may make you fat. Consuming spectacularly excessive quantities may, in fact, make you clinically obese or, in plain English, so incredibly fat that short people huddle under your blubber as shade on hot days. Also, eating these food substances may contribute to diabetes, cancer, heart disease, blindness, deafness, numbness, and tingling in limbs. You may have allergic reactions to these food substances. You may choke on a sandwich [like Mama Cass]. In short, eating can kill you any number of ways. It is a dangerous and harmful thing to do. If you consume food substances in this establishment identified as "dessert," these warnings are treble true. Especially dangerous and potentially harmful are desserts identified on our menu as "Chocolate Death Cake" (hint, hint, hint) and "Banana Fudge Mountain." We make no representations whatsoever as to the nutritional value of the food substances we serve; to the contrary, it is our opinion that the food substances we serve have no redeeming nutritional value at all. Further, certain of the food substances we serve have ingredients and/or combinations of ingredients that may be or may in the future be judged to be addictive. The owners of, investors in, employees of, landlord of,

FIGURE 2.1: Legal Document, continued

and vendors to this establishment accept absolutely no responsibility or liability for whatever results you may experience as a result of eating here, including but not limited to, obesity and related adverse health conditions. If you have any concerns about these matters, please use your pudgy fingers to push the buttons on your cell phone and consult your physician and/or attorney before eating.

WAIVER OF LIABILITY

"I, _____, hereby acknowledge that I have read the above Legal Notice carefully and understand it completely, and I certify that I am not an idiot. Further, I warrant that I will not, in any way, at any time, attempt to hold this establishment responsible or liable for any health or medical conditions I may have or develop in the future, including but not limited to obesity and related conditions. I also hereby prohibit any member of my family or any other individual, organization, or entity from attempting to hold this establishment responsible or liable as noted above on my behalf. I firmly and clearly state that I am fully and completely responsible for whatever I pick up and stick into my pie hole."

Signature: _____

Print Name: _____

Witness Signature: _____

Witness Name: _____

FIGURE **2.1:** Legal Document, continued

Disclaimer: This document is provided for entertainment purposes only, is not intended as a substitute for actual legal advice, and should you need a legal document for this or any other purpose, the services of a competent legal professional should be sought. Its author and/or publisher accepts no responsibility or liability for your use or misuse of this document provided for entertainment purposes only.

From: www.dankennedy.com

CHAPTER 3

How Do You Know If You
Have a Really Good Idea?

*A hunting party was hopelessly lost, deep in the woods.
"I thought you were the best guide in all of Canada,"
complained one of the hunters. "I am," said the
guide, "but I think we're in Michigan now."*

The late Wilson Harrell, entrepreneur and business consultant, had a unique way of testing a new product, service, or business idea. He called it the "Well, I'll be damned!" test. Harrell suggested taking a sample of your idea to at least 20 potential buyers (but not friends, relatives, or neighbors!) to see how they would react. If they didn't say, "Well, I'll be damned" or "Why didn't I think of that?" he did not have a winner.

If most of the people do say the magic words, ask them other questions such as: What would you be willing to pay for this? If it were available at that price, would you definitely buy it? Maybe buy it? Why? How would you use it? Do you think it's such a good idea you might want to invest in it? Why? Why not?

He described a loose type of "focus group," and it does have value. Even better, I've encouraged inventors to get even a primitive version of their product made, then set up at a swap meet, grab a microphone hooked to a loudspeaker, and try to sell the product, just like the slicer-dicer guy does at the county fair. If you can't sell it there, you probably can't sell it on TV or in print ads or off store shelves either.

The point is that one way or another you have to get an assessment from the actual marketplace, preferably early rather than late, at as little cost as possible.

This brings us to the most important rule of entrepreneurial marketing I can imagine.

Dan Kennedy's
Eternal Truth #5

You cannot trust your own
judgment. Test, test, test.
Then test some more.

Are entrepreneurs impatient by nature? Maybe so, but successful entrepreneurs must learn to be patient sometimes. Testing is one of those times. Any time you can, any way you can, test.

Ask Your Customers

At Stew Leonard's famous supermarket (www.stewleonards.com), management regularly meets with groups of customers over coffee and doughnuts to ask them what they like, what they don't like, what they'd like done differently, and what they think of a new product or service. One giant sales breakthrough, which was written about in detail in Tom Peters' original edition of *In Search of Excellence,* came from such meetings.

A major electronics and appliance retailer took the trouble of finding out what his stores' customers liked best and least about buying televisions, stereos, and appliances. One comment was so frequent it stood out like the proverbial sore thumb: people hated having to block a whole day out of their schedules to wait around for the delivery of what they had purchased. So he developed a system to provide scheduled delivery times guaranteed within a two-hour range. This service became his main advertising promise, with fantastic results!

My clients who market information to niche industries, such as the publishers of courses, books, tapes, and newsletters for chiropractors, dentists, carpet cleaners, auto repair shop owners, photography studio owners, independent pharmacies, and so on, have learned the value of frequently surveying their customers. They probe for unmet needs, unfulfilled desires, new frustrations, and then they create the information product that matches up. I call this "build to suit" product development.

Ask Your Counterparts and Competitors

One of the easiest, quickest research tasks every business owner must do is to go to the library, get Yellow Pages directories from other major cities, and look through all the advertising in your category of business. You'll inevitably find advertisers somewhere doing something nobody in your area is doing, and that should give you some good new ideas. You may also find somebody offering a product or service that you have considered; it won't hurt to call that businessperson and discuss experiences. You might even go visit the business.

The same holds true for your competitors. You probably can't have a direct talk with them, but you can check up on them. I'm amazed at the businesspeople who never go to their competitors' stores or buy their products.

Smart Direct-Mail Testing

One of my earlier books, *The Ultimate Sales Letter,* is all about how to create good direct-mail campaigns and sales letters, even if you know nothing about writing. I wrote that book because I believe direct mail is the very best way most entrepreneurs have available for marketing their products and services, for the simple reason that it is the easiest to test results.

Other types of advertising are much more difficult to test. How do you test a Yellow Pages ad, for example? That same ad is stuck there for 12 months; you can't change it. The most frustrating thing about producing TV infomercials is the inability to test different ideas, promises, and offers without actually putting together different shows at great expense.

Direct mail offers the unique opportunity to do cheap testing. You can tell a lot from tests as small as a few hundred pieces mailed, depending on the market, lists used, and other factors. This means you can "split-test" one letter against another or one offer, price, or premium against another, for just a few hundred dollars. And, once you find a campaign that works, you can keep on testing other variables cheaply and easily to try and make it better. Best of all, once you find that success formula, you will probably be able to use it to get consistent, successful results for years.

In recent years, other media offering easy and fast split-test opportunities have evolved. If you have a customer or prospect list with e-mail addresses or fax numbers and the customers' or prospects' permission to contact them (or you can joint venture with someone who does), you can conduct a decent split-test dirt cheap in one day's time. It is easy to set up two clone Web sites— each making an identical offer but with different prices or each identical except for two different headlines—do an e-mail "blast" inviting people to the site and directing every other visitor to the alternating sites. Similarly, you can build a fax, change one variable, and fax half your list Version #1, half Version #2.

In many instances, if I am trying to first test the premise only; (*are they interested in 'x')?*, I'll offer some kind of free report, tape, sample, etc. rather than try to sell an actual product. If prospects won't respond to get it for free, they probably won't pay for it either. This allows you to "dry-test." For the most part, dry-testing, i.e., offering a product for sale before it has actually been produced and inventoried for instant delivery, is illegal. By giving away something free that does exist, you avoid the costs of producing products that may not be saleable, so you legally dry-test.

"Steal" Already-Tested Direct Marketing Strategies

But what if you can't test? First of all, you need to know as much as you can about what works and what doesn't in your particular business. You need to do your homework on your industry, your counterparts, your competitors, and your customers. Simply, the more you know, the better your "guess."

Let me tell you a secret. I get paid a great deal of money to "create" brilliant marketing ideas, but I doubt that I've ever honestly done that. Inventing a new idea is a lot of work. Stealing a successful idea is a lot faster, easier, and more likely to yield successful results. So, I try to legally "steal" whenever I can.

For example, I was recently hired to write a full-page magazine ad for a money-making opportunity, so I needed a "killer" headline. I found the two most successful ads I had seen for other money-making opportunities, took the best parts of each, and combined them into a new headline. Then I changed the details to match my client's offer. This ad is working like gangbusters.

> I am a highly paid direct-response copywriter, typically commanding $15,000.00 to as much as $70,000.00 plus royalties to write an ad, sales letter, or direct-mail campaign. More than 85% of all the clients who use me once do so again. As you might guess, there's a very, very small fraternity of pro copywriters at this fee level. Most of us know each other well. I can tell you with authority, we all use these kinds of "swipe files," to efficiently recycle what we know works, rather than to invent from scratch and experiment unnecessarily.

The headline creation process took me 20 minutes. To have thought it up from scratch could have taken 20 hours.

A friend with a specialty retail store came to me in need of an idea to stimulate a fast surge of cash flow. Fortunately, he had a mailing list of his past customers, so he could get the job done with a great sales letter. I pulled the perfect letter out of my files, one that a chiropractor had used to promote a "patient appreciation" event, and said, "Here, sit down and rewrite this letter. Don't change much except the details for your products." It took him only one hour to compose a letter that brought in more than $30,000.00 in 15 days.

Given the right resources, you can go a long way on 100% borrowed, already-proven strategies.

Moving Ideas from One Business to Another

To the best of my knowledge, the drive-up service window belonged to the banking industry before anybody else latched on to it. But it sure does account for a lot of the fast-food industry sales. It is also used by dry cleaners, beverage stores, video rental stores, and florists. In Las Vegas, one casino has a drive-up betting window for sports bettors. Others that I haven't noticed probably use it and still others could and should use it.

Somebody in the fast-food business "stole" this idea. My vision is of a McDonald's executive sitting in his car in the bank drive-in line on Friday afternoon when it hits him—"Hey, I don't think we can fit the milkshakes in the little tube, but outside of that, this could work for us!"

Just about every idea came from something already created or used. The very successful *Amazing Discoveries* format for TV

One of the most successful borrowed strategies I've dealt with recently has to do with what we call a "better your best contest." I first paid attention to it when—along with my client and friend Joe Polish—I was doing some consulting work for the giant nutrition company, EAS, then owned by Bill Phillips.

Bill is a brilliant, innovative, and aggressive entrepreneur. He had fueled dramatic growth of his company by promoting a contest with exciting prizes, including cars and trips, for people who used his products to lose weight and build better bodies. They competed against their own "before's"; winning was based on best improvement more than competition with others.

Joe and I liked it so well that, a year later, we created a similar contest for the carpet cleaners that Joe works with, offering an array of prizes, including Joe's own Jaguar, to cleaning company operators who created the greatest improvements in their businesses using Joe's systems. In 2003, hundreds competed in Joe's contest, and the top prize of a shiny new Hummer was given away. I have two other clients for whom we've copied the idea and created comparable contests with great results in each case. So a contest designed for body-builders becomes a contest to motivate carpet cleaners, chiropractors, and investment advisors to make improvements in their businesses.

infomercials was a cross between a game show and a state fair barker demonstrating the magic slicer-dicer to a gathered crowd. Club Med is a cruise ship set up on land. *Star Wars* was an updated version of the classic western movie.

I tell entrepreneurs they will rarely, if ever, find the basis for a big breakthrough in their business or income inside their own industry or profession. Breakthroughs come from outside.

How to Be More "Creative"

I use the word *creative* with caution.

Twyla Tharp is an extremely talented woman. She won two Tony Awards recently for a narrative dance play based on Billy Joel's music. Over a 40-year career, she has invented 125 different dances. Unfortunately for unwary or easily influenced businesspeople, she has now written a business book, *The Creative Habit: Learn It and Use It for Life*. I say *unfortunately* because she is all about the exact kind of creativity best kept out of business. The article in *Fast Company* about her begins with these words:

> *Creativity starts with a blank space. She says, "The blank space can be humbling."*

This kind of creativity is wonderful, awe-inspiring, and produces groundbreaking art, literature, and theater. But if you're after maximum profits with minimum time and minimum agony, it has no place in business. And when it comes to your advertising and marketing, that goes double—avoid this notion like the plague for two simple reasons. One, it is horribly inefficient— she's right; the blank page is a problem and should be avoided. Two, it is experimental; there's no need for experimentation with your marbles when there's abundant opportunity to achieve your every objective without it.

For business purposes, focus on "practical creativity." Mike Vance talks about it in terms of re-arranging the old (i.e., tested and proven) in a new way, or "plus-ing" what already works. Either way, you're not starting with a blank page. Walt Disney didn't start Disneyland with a blank page; he started with already proven, profitable amusement parks and began subtracting things he disliked and adding things he thought could be done better, further plus-ing new ideas on top of the re-arranged old ones. Alex Osborne, a dean of creativity, filled his book with checklists to facilitate re-arranging the old in new ways. I talk about this in terms of bringing something from outside your field that is proven elsewhere into your field. Or cutting and pasting from swipe files, whether stored in file cabinets or your subconscious. But you'll never hear me talk in terms of starting with a blank slate. And catching me starting anything with a blank page is a rare event.

For purely artistic expression, raw, out of the ether creativity may be an essential ingredient. But for commercial purposes, it is vastly overrated. Even if you look at the movie industry, as a quote-creative-unquote business, when you examine the biggest box office successes of at least the past decade, you'll find very, very, very few to be original, birthed from the blank slate. Many have been remakes of previously successful films. Some have featured well-established, successful, known characters from comic books, TV shows, or sequels. A movie such as *Star Wars* is merely a classic western with a shiny new wrapping on it.

Let's examine a few places you might get "beginnings," so you need not begin with the blank page.

Competitors

Direct competitors occasionally have good ideas badly executed.
You should keep a close eye on competitors, as well as on leaders of your field outside your geographic market. You ought to
keep a file on each of these, making sure you have their ads, mailings, etc. Visit their stores or showrooms, call, and "play
prospect" at their offices. *Practice Coach & others.*

Comparables Help Menial – coach reps

This is my number-one source of good, raw material. A "compa- in lieu
rable" is someone selling a totally different, completely uncom- of them
petitive product or service but selling at your price point and/or promoting
to your customers and/or using the same media you use. If you me.
ferret out successful comparables and carefully follow them, sponsoring
you'll often find terrific shortcuts. Just for example, I've told a cosmetic dentist who wants affluent patients from all over the coun- seminars
try to fly in for his services that he should "play prospect" and Can help
answer the full-page ads run in airline magazines by the carpal
tunnel doctors in Texas and by the Mayo Clinic for its Executive improving
Program. These are not competitors, but they are comparable in market
many ways: the clientele, the geographic reach, pricing, the same penetration
marketing challenge, etc. Set a goal to find, thoroughly research, for their
and build a file on one new comparable a month. You'll thank me. products.

News

News events beget opportunities, based on the principle taught
by the legendary copywriter Robert Collier of entering the conversation already going on in the public's or prospect's mind.
When Arnold Schwarzenegger was running for governor in
California, in a contest with some 50 other candidates, Taco Bell

quickly capitalized with an ad campaign and promotion where the major candidates were represented by different menu items. You cast your vote by purchasing. I encourage my clients to have a "rapid response plan" in place, like politicians do, to quickly pounce on the opportunities presented by timely news events. Then use these events as fodder for communication with their clientele and as a basis for sales, events, ad campaigns, or publicity.

Old Ads

Go back 10, 20, 30 years, take big winners, and recycle them. I use my swipe file of these "classics" more than I use current samples.

Top Direct-Response Copywriters' Work

If you're going to crib, crib from the best. Look for direct-response ads full of copy, running repeatedly in national media—from *USA Today* to *National Enquirer* to niche magazines. Often a good ad that has nothing whatsoever to do with your business can still provide a "platform" to work on (rather than a blank slate). This is why you should scan magazines far outside your personal interests on a frequent basis.

This is just a brief, partial sampling of ways to avoid the blank page. And you must avoid that at all costs.

Creativity Formulas

Most entrepreneurial fortunes are made *without* brand-new ideas. Instead, entrepreneurs tend to alter, combine, and "twist" proven winners. Here are a few of the creativity formulas for getting this done. Look for these or other principles behind everything you encounter. Pretty soon this will be a habit of thinking, and you'll automatically be more creative!

If You Can't Change the Product, Change the Package

Cheeseburgers. With bacon, without bacon. Round, Square. Now what? After just about everything that could be done to a cheeseburger had been done to a cheeseburger, McDonald's created the McDLT. Remember? "Keeps the hot side hot, the cold side, cold." The product stayed the same; the package changed. I always liked this package gimmick. If you expand this idea to *"change the positioning,"* you'll have a more recent fast-food industry example: Subway's repositioning of its giant, stuffed sandwiches as a weight-loss plan, ala Jared.

Make It Bigger

Big screen TVs, "home theaters." Gilleys, once the largest country-western night club in America. 7-11's Big Gulp. The Ford Expedition. The Hummer. "Family size" frozen dinners.

Make It Smaller

How about a TV that fits in your pocket? One-serving sizes of pudding, yogurt, microwavable spaghetti.

Add to It

Shampoo plus conditioner in one. Cold capsules enriched with vitamin C. A bookstore-cafe combination. Lee Iacocca told me that the first minivan was an exercise in selling $20,000.00 cupholders. Now cars are being sold because of DVD players, GPS navigational systems, and GM's OnStar service—the car itself is secondary to what has been added!

Subtract from It

The convertible (a top-less car). Foods with no preservatives. No Appointment Hair Cutters, a successful, national, no-frills chain of salons.

Do It Faster
The ten-minute oil change. Speed-dialers for telephones. The microwave oven—once thought salable only to restaurants, by the way. High-speed Internet vs. dial-up.

Do It Slower
The car wash by hand. Vacation travel by train.

Do It Cheaper
Cubic zirconia jewelry. Wal-Mart.

Do It More Expensively
The Neiman Marcus Christmas catalog, filled with very pricey, unique gifts, gets millions of dollars of free publicity every year. First-class air travel. The pricier Four Seasons Hotel inside the Mandalay Bay resort in Las Vegas.

The savviest entrepreneurs I work with compile, keep, and frequently use checklists like this one, as on-demand brainstorming partners they don't have to pay.

What If Everybody Hates Your Idea?

A lot of very smart people did nothing but discourage Walt Disney. A lot of very smart people told Dave Thomas the fast-food hamburger business was saturated. I'm sure we could fill a whole shelf full of books with similar examples. There's probably a product in every room of the house that was once criticized as a dumb idea.

My Platinum Inner Circle group is a mastermind and peer advisory group made up exclusively of information marketers. About four or five years ago, Reed Hoisington, a Member who provides information, seminars, and services to mortgage brokers, proposed a radical change in the way he would charge for his continuing monthly services. In essence, he had decided to force the buyers of one of his single, stand-alone products to also sign up for an automatic monthly shipment of more information and an automatic monthly credit card charge. His customer would be unable to do one without the other, unable to buy Item A without agreeing to accept a monthly continuing commitment. There's a term for this: forced continuity.

The guy getting paid the big bucks to advise everybody—me—argued against this idea.

It was my opinion that this strategy, depicted on the order form, would suppress response and that it would later cause massive confusion, customer service problems, and refund demands as customers started getting "dinged" each month on their credit cards but didn't remember agreeing to the charges. Most of the other Platinum Members agreed with me. If this had been a committee in a big company, our "no" vote would have killed the idea.

Fortunately for all of us, Reed ignored us and went ahead and did exactly what he had proposed. This probably reflects his long experience of ignoring what he has been told and doing what he pleases.

Anyway, five months later, at our next meeting, he had gloriously positive results and few problems to report. Still skeptical, several other members carefully tested the idea in their businesses. Within a year, we were all using it one way or another. My very conservative estimate of money lost personally by not knowing about this process and doing it ten years ago is $5 million, net. In virtually every case, it has boosted sales and profits and dramatically improved retention in subscription-type products, as well as eliminated the costly task of renewal marketing.

Once my service has good recognition I will tie it to monthly services, at additional cost.

If you really have faith in your idea, even if no one else does, and you go in with your eyes open knowing you may lose, then—charge! On the other hand, keep in mind that the true entrepreneur marries goals and objectives, not isolated ideas. When one of your ideas does prove itself unprofitable, don't try to raise the dead; move on to the next method of achieving your goals. The entrepreneurial graveyard is full of corpses of exhausted individuals so emotionally married to a bad idea they marched stubbornly on to starvation. Persistence in and of itself is vastly overrated. Used in proper context, persistence is a virtue. Glorified and adhered to without qualification, it is a deadly vice.

In 1941, 8th-grade dropout and bakery delivery man Carl Karcher mortgaged his car for $350.00 to buy a hot dog stand. His first day's sales were an unexciting $14.75. But, by 1946, more hot dog stands followed; then hamburgers and "Carl's special sauce" were added. Today, the Carl's Jr. chain includes more than 400 restaurants, all based on serving a top-quality hamburger. The unique factor is what Carl calls "partial hostess service." His are the only fast-food joints where you place your order, sit down with your beverages, and wait for an employee to bring your fresh-cooked food to you, rather than standing around waiting at the counter.

But around 1983, Carl had a bright idea that didn't work out. Like all fast-food places, the bulk of the business was breakfast and lunch. Carl decided to buck that norm and go after the family dinner business. He introduced new charbroiled dinner platters—steak, chicken and fish—at all the restaurants and invested heavily in advertising and promoting these new items to woo customers in at dinner hour. Even the signs on all the locations were changed from Carl's Jr. Charbroiled Hamburgers to Carl's

Jr. Restaurant. Millions of dollars were poured into this new approach.

Instead of adding revenue, the dinner idea confused franchisees, managers, and the public. Average annual sales per location dropped. In 1985, Carl Karcher had to face up to the fact that his Big Idea was a flop. He dug in and started leading his company back to its reliable roots. The signs were changed back, menus simplified, prices cut, and the advertising spotlight returned to the famous charbroiled hamburgers. Sales almost immediately started climbing.

At the time, Carl Karcher told *Nation's Business* magazine, "The stress these last several years has probably been greater than at any time in my life. When you've put in 45 years, you think that everything's going to get easier. Nothing is easy! And I think that's where too many people fail in business—they think they've got it made. It's fun being in business, but there's no rest for the wicked."

---

*O*n (only) two occasions in 25 years, I have stubbornly refused to listen to what the marketplace was desperately trying to tell me, poured a lot of good money after bad, and invested untold quantities of time and energy into proverbially beating the clearly dead horse. The details of these situations aren't important and are a bit painful and embarrassing to tell. No one is immune to such overcommitment.

Carl Karcher has certainly had many good business ideas during his career, and he has backed those ideas with his faith and with action. But as his story shows, nobody gets by without having a clinker now and again. You will too. So, go ahead, have the guts to act on those you really believe in—and the good sense to walk away from those that prove unrewarding.

In the direct marketing world where I mostly live, we do not even speak in terms of "success" or "failure" with regard to ads, sales letters, infomercials, or marketing campaigns. The word *failure* tends to inflame the stubborn streak in entrepreneurs, too often leading to the aforementioned beating of dead horses. Instead, we talk only in terms of "tests."

This is the soundest approach to everything entrepreneurial. Condition yourself to think tests, not failures or successes. Then make it your priority to test fast and cheap, drop like hot potatoes ideas that test poorly, and move on to the next test. Ultimately, this is the only way to determine whether you have a good idea or not.

There's even danger in the terms *good* and *bad*. An idea may be a good idea but still inappropriate for you to invest resources in, depending on how it fits with your major goals and objectives, your skills and talents. An idea might be good for one company but bad for another. Just because it's a great opportunity does not mean it's a great opportunity—or the best opportunity at this moment—for you. Because there is no shortage of opportunity, the entrepreneur has to be selective.

Get book on sales letters, direct marketing.

CHAPTER 4

Positioning Yourself
and Your Business for
Maximum Success

If you don't think advertising works, consider the
millions of people who now think yogurt tastes good.

—Bob Orben

ositioning is admittedly an advertising buzzword, but it's
legitimately one of the most important marketing concepts you'll ever consider in your entrepreneurial career.
One of the definitions of positioning is controlling how your customers and prospective customers think and feel about your
business in comparison to other, similar businesses competing
for their attention.

I have several specific suggestions about this process. Maybe
they'll seem obvious to you, but I can tell you that I have seen
many businesspeople overlook the obvious and cost themselves
a lot of money as a result.

Positioning Strategy #1: How to Name What You Do to Attract the Customers You Want

Let's start with the name of your business. I insist the best business name telegraphs what the business does. This may sound elementary. But start looking at the businesses in your town, and notice how many of their names, boldly displayed on their signs, do *not* instantly tell you what the business offers and does. There is a large chain of art and craft supply stores called Michaels. For years, its signage said only Michaels. Recently, I noticed new signs: *Michael's Arts and Crafts*. I'll bet they finally discovered something.

Think of the instant print industry. For many years, there were three large U.S. chains named Postal Instant Press, Sir Speedy, and Kwik Kopy. In the case of Sir Speedy, the name is not a marketing advantage and may be a disadvantage. Couldn't Sir Speedy be a dry cleaners? A quick lube shop? A messenger service? Kwik Kopy gets the same issue of speed into its name while better describing what it does, but many people think of Kwik Kopy only as a source of copies, not quality printing. For years, my brother had a shop, General Graphics and Printing, located very close to a Kwik Kopy. He got many customers who had photocopies made at Kwik Kopy but brought their larger printing jobs to him, not realizing that both shops were basically the same. Postal Instant Press would have been a much better name had all the chain's shops been located near post offices.

Of course, all these chains were successful, but you have to ask yourself: could they have been more successful with a clearer identity? If you were entering that industry, is there a name that would give you a competitive edge?

The instant print business has had a huge turnover of players since I wrote the first edition of this book. The aforementioned

Names such as Dunkin' Donuts, Midas Mufflers, Domino's Pizza Delivers, and Minute-Lube are all good examples of names that serve as marketing tools. I think it was a classic case of big corporate stupidity when, after Quaker State bought Minute-Lube, they spent a fortune converting colors at all the locations from red and yellow to green and changing the name Minute-Lube to Q-Lube. From a name that telegraphs the service to a name that means nothing.

chains still exist, but Kinkos has surpassed them all—in spite, in my opinion, of a truly terrible name, which it offsets with a number of other positive factors, including superior technology and a self-serve environment. Kinkos did for copying what Piggly Wiggly did for grocery stores decades before. I still wonder how much more successful Kinkos might be or how much faster it might have grown with a better name.

Names can help with positioning. Consider Emergency Chiropractic or Chronic Pain Control Center. Both are names of chiropractic practices. One targets accident victims, the other targets people with long-term, recurring problems. When you develop your business name, product names, and service names, think in terms of telegraphing, of targeting, and of giving yourself a marketing advantage.

Some years back, I was asked to develop a name for a weed-killing product in an aerosol can. I wound up with Kills Weeds

Dead. Do you have any doubt about what the product does? Isn't that name a lot better than Formula 42X?

Titles Matter

A lot. I have fought with all my publishers over my own book titles, except this publisher, which cheerfully accepted the long, awkward title and "No B.S." positioning. That *is* my position; I have cultivated a reputation as a blunt, direct "no B.S." individual. Anyway, titles matter beyond the book business. Titles or names are important for products and for offers.

For example, should a restaurant have "New Fall Menu Items" or "New Fall Flavor Adventures"? The naming of menu items is so vitally important in the restaurant industry that Rory Fatt, my Platinum Member and CEO of Restaurant Marketing Systems Inc., and I developed a complete, interactive checklist and questionnaire on CD-ROM to help restaurant owners brainstorm.

Someone once told me about seeing a sign for an upcoming free seminar titled "12 Roadblocks to Financial Success" and concluding he had no need to attend—because he already knew more than 12!

Maybe he was joking. Maybe not. But the seminar's attraction certainly would have been improved by adding "How to Overcome" to its title.

I have a Member in the photography business who split-tested via direct mail a particular offer, altering only the name of the offer. Version One was "Family Portrait Mothers' Day Gift"; Version Two was "The Ultimate Mothers' Day Gift: The Family Portrait." Version Two outpulled Version One in responses by better than a 3-to-1 margin, a 300% difference.

Labeling the Process

Finally, there is the naming or titling of your "process." You can more clearly communicate and add value to what you do solely by enhancing its name. For example, The 10-Minute Oil Change is perceived differently if it's The 9-Minute Oil Change, the Guaranteed 10-Minute Oil Change, or the Indy 500-Style 10-Minute Oil Change.

My client Joe Polish, of Piranha Marketing, invented "The Carpet Audit" to describe the process the carpet cleaners he trains go through when first coming to your home. This is actually the calculation of the price you'll pay to have your carpets cleaned, but he "dressed up" the process itself by having the cleaner go through the house putting different colored stickers on different stains and engaging in other visible diagnostics. By doing so and giving it a name, he is able to advertise and market the Free Carpet Audit as something of value, interest, and benefit.

Positioning Strategy #2: How to Price

You'll hear a lot of different opinions about pricing strategy. Personally, I don't think I'd ever want to be in a business that procured its customers with the lure of "lowest prices." You cannot build long-term customer retention via the cheapest price.

The way you get a customer has great impact on how you will sell to that customer again. There will always be someone willing to offer a cheaper price. If the only thing binding your customers to your company is the lowest price, your business will be as fragile in its tenth year as in its tenth week.

In every business I'm involved in, we sell quality, value, service, and unique benefits. We do not sell price.

It's helpful to use the supply-and-demand concept in commanding high prices or fees. In my own speaking and consulting business, the busier I've become, the more selective I've become about accepting clients and projects; and, in recent years, I've been striving to reduce travel. Altogether, this has created a greater demand than supply of me. Because I'm busy and rarely in the office, it may be days, even a week or so, before somebody new is able to connect with me. Then I'll check a schedule that may not have room for a meeting for weeks. Even telephone calls have to be scheduled in advance as appointments. For me, this has all proven beneficial. The less available I am, the more I seem to be wanted and appreciated.

So here's a big, big success secret: find ways to create exclusivity, to portray greater demand than supply.

I also believe that the most stable markets are linked to the highest quality. One of my favorite companies is Omaha Steaks, a thriving mail-order firm. You can buy steaks for less money just about anywhere, but you can't buy better steaks. Its customer service is outstanding, and customer retention is extraordinarily high. The "low end" of that same market has virtually no loyalty, moves from one grocery store to the other, moved by cheap-price coupons in the newspaper. Which type of customer base would you rather have?

Actually, customer "loyalty" is a misnomer, a commonly used term but also an illusion. There was a day when a "Ford man" was a "Ford man" for life, and he would nearly get into a fistfight with a "Chevy man" defending his preference. He wouldn't dream of buying another brand of car. Those days are gone. Today, businesses incessantly have to earn repeat business and customer retention. You cannot earn it by cheap price because someone will always be willing to go cheaper, even if it kills them.

The worst thing for any business, for any provider is "commoditization," being perceived as an interchangeable commodity. When you sell by emphasizing cheap price, you invite that perception.

Another interesting thing about price is how fearful most business owners are of raising prices or offering premium-priced options. **Here's a scary thought**: you are selling everything you sell for less than you need to. **Scarier thought**: you're selling less of it at lower prices than you would at higher prices.

What They Don't Know . . .

One of the longest running game shows on TV is Bob Barker's *The Price Is Right,* where contestants try to guess the correct prices of mostly common, frequently purchased items—and they often are wrong by 50% or more. This is real reality TV, revealing the fact that consumers do not know what items they routinely buy are supposed to cost, which you should take as assurance they are clueless about things that are only occasional, unusual purchases. In other words, they judge whether your price is "too high" or not based *NOT* on any knowledge of their own, but *SOLELY* on how you present it.

There's a lengthy article about this in the September 2003 issue of *Harvard Business Review*, which includes citing a university study that had researchers in supermarkets ask consumers to price objects as they put them in their shopping carts. Less than half got them right. As a caution, most underestimated the price. I say "caution" because I believe this reinforces your task of *selling* premium prices.

> The most important lesson is that price is NOT linked to your prospect's actual knowledge of what the price should be or what comparable prices are. You have far more freedom and flexibility than you probably take advantage of to price as you please.

Of course, there are consumers who research prices of major purchases via the Internet, *Consumer Reports,* and simple price shopping. Most recent stats I've seen indicate this involves less than 10% of the marketplace, and most research is limited to cars, major appliances, swimming pools, and about a dozen other big purchases. If you sacrifice them all, there's 90% left. Further, you should be selling in a self-created competitive vacuum, where price is evaluated by the prospect only against value, only based on your presentation, not in a competitive arena, price to price. In other words, *the more effectively you do your marketing job as I teach, the less price matters.*

#1 Myth and Fear about Raising Prices

The *Harvard Business Review* article also dispels the commonly held belief that raising prices adversely affects sales. This is not always true. In one case, a women's clothing catalog increased demand for a dress by raising the price from $34 to $39, but changing from $34 to $44 had no effect. So, two things: the 9 seemed like a better value than the 4, even though it raised the price by $5.00. However, there might be more net profit selling fewer at $44 than selling more at $39.

A Few Other Pricing Strategies

For professional practices, I often suggest "differential pricing." For example, if you want my coaching group Member, lawyer Mace Yampolsky, to *personally handle* your DUI case, the rate is X dollars an hour; OR if you want one of the firm's other lawyers, *supervised* by Mace, to handle it, the fee is less, only Y dollars per hour. This works for doctors, dentists, chiropractors, lawyers, CPAs, etc., but can conceivably have wider application.

My client and Platinum Member Mike Storms is a great example of a premium price marketer. His Mike Storms Karate is located in a small town in Louisiana, with nine—count 'em nine—competing schools all within stone's throw distance. All nine have cheaper prices than Mike whose fees are two to five times higher than these nearby competitors. Yet Mike's school has grown by double digit percentages year after year, is very high in national rankings, and enjoys exceptional retention and referral rates. How can this be?

There are many factors, although none have to do with the core product being delivered. It would take a whole book by itself to detail all the contributing factors, but here are three big, nontechnical ones: Mike's decision to deliberately be the highest priced provider; Mike's total lack of concern about competitors' discounting; and Mike's overall positioning strategy communicated throughout his advertising, marketing, location, and school environment, etc. so that he attracts clients who make buying decisions based on merits other than lowest price.

No, this is not to say you can't succeed carving out the lowest price position; obviously you can't argue with Wal-Mart's success. It is, however, a much more dangerous place to be than at the premium price end of the spectrum. On the surface, it may seem like the path of least resistance to cut prices, to be cheaper. But to do so, you will sacrifice margin, be more restricted in what you can invest to acquire customers and in what you can do to satisfy them once you have them, and you'll always be vulnerable to low-price competition.

Whatever you decide about price, recognize you are dealing with something bigger and more important than just price; you are positioning your business in a particular place.

Positioning Strategy #3: How to Make Your Image Work for You

As long as I live, I will never forget a bank manager looking me straight in the eye and in a genuinely sincere, shocked voice saying, "You can't be president of a company—you're not wearing a tie." To be perceived, without risk of exception, as a successful entrepreneur, you must match the image of a successful entrepreneur. To be perceived, without risk of exception, as successful and trustworthy in your field, you must match the image of a successful person in your field.

Places of business, product packaging, literature, and advertising are all subject to the same image concerns as are individuals' appearances. Whether I walk on stage in a suit or in jeans has nothing to do with the quality or value of the speech I'll deliver, but it will have everything to do with how that speech is received. If I come on in the jeans, I instantly create psychological obstacles to acceptance. I've proven to myself that the most authoritative look makes a difference. At most of my speaking engagements, I sell my books and cassettes. I tested, with identical types of audiences, tie, sport coat, and slacks vs. light-colored suit vs. dark navy or black, pinstriped suit, and I always enjoyed greater sales with the last "look."

Dan Kennedy's Eternal Truth #7

We're taught that you can't judge a book by its cover, but we can't help but judge a book by its cover. You will be judged that way, too.

Is this fair? Of course not. It, unfortunately, allows racist, sexist, and other prejudices to live on. And you can certainly have a lot of moral outrage over it if you want to.

But I'm going to ask you a defining question: would you rather be right or rich? I call this a defining question for entrepreneurs because it challenges you to be totally realistic and pragmatic, give up your excuses, and succeed. A lot of people would rather live mediocre lives under the protection of the "it's not fair" excuse umbrella than to face the world as it really is and do what is necessary to win. A lot of people will cling to certain beliefs and behaviors even at the expense of desirable results. The most successful entrepreneurs I know are willing to change their beliefs and behaviors whenever that change can facilitate the most desirable results.

Now, don't misunderstand. I'm not suggesting the politicians' chameleon game, changing minute by minute, audience by audience, dressing up for one group, down for the next, telling anybody and everybody what they want to hear with no regard for truth or contradiction, with no core philosophy other than the desired results. There has to be a "you" in there somewhere. There has to be a collection of core values not subject to easy change. But there are many things not nearly as important as core values that can be easily modified to permit success.

I once counseled a struggling attorney who couldn't understand why he wasn't attracting or keeping solid business clients. The day he drove me from his office to a lunch meeting in his canary-yellow, four-year-old pickup truck, I told him why. Of course, he protested mightily. He loved his truck, it was paid for, it shouldn't matter. But his practice started picking up when he started driving a Cadillac.

On the other hand, with regard to advertising or literature or direct mail, I must strongly caution you against image over substance. All too often, marketing material is pretty (and expensive) but fails to deliver a compelling direct-response message. Most businesses are better served by thinking about their marketing tools as "salesmanship in media" rather than as "advertising." In simple terms, copy is king. Message matters most. Yes, the wrong presentation for a given market can sabotage even the best message. But the more common error is a beautiful presentation of—nothing.

Positioning Strategy #4: Self-Appointments

When we are kids, our parents "appoint us" old enough to stay home alone, old enough to babysit our younger brothers or sisters, old enough to date, and so on. At work, employers or supervisors "promote us." In all these experiences, there is someone else, some authority figure, determining that you are qualified to do a certain thing or handle a certain responsibility. This conditioning is not particularly useful when you step into the entrepreneurial world.

People often ask me, "How do you become a professional speaker?" They're looking for some kind of organized path such as going to a school, passing tests, and, finally, getting appointed as a professional by some kind of group. They're disappointed when I say, "Be one."

Early in my career, I read Robert Ringer's book *Winning Through Intimidation,* which made me understand that the biggest problem with getting to the top is getting through the crowd at the bottom. Ringer suggested simply "leap-frogging" over them. I've done that all my life. But I notice most people waiting around for someone else to recognize them, to give them permission to be successful.

Please understand, *you do not need anybody's permission to be successful.* And, if you wait for "the establishment" in any given field to grant you that permission, you'll wait a long, long time. And remember, success is never an accident, no matter how it appears to outsiders.

Jay Leno got Johnny Carson's job, arguably the best job in show business. At one time, comedian Gary Shandling was considered the front-runner for that job, and David Letterman was after it, too. But only Leno quietly went out and appointed himself to the job. In his travels, he went to the local NBC affiliates in different cities and towns, befriended the station managers, did promotional spots for them for free, and operated as the self-appointed ambassador of goodwill for the network and the show. By the time Carson retired, Leno was the only candidate with the solid support of all the NBC affiliates. Who told him he could do this? Nobody. He just did it.

"Expert positioning" is all about self-appointment, self-promotion and self-aggrandizement. Years ago, a client of mine, Dr. Robert Kotler, a Beverly Hills cosmetic surgeon, wrote and self-published a book titled *The Consumer's Guide to Cosmetic Surgery.* He has since been able to promote himself as *the* doctor who wrote *the* book.

Years ago, relatively early in my speaking career, I got an important invitation to speak at the lunch meetings of the prestigious CEO Clubs, made up exclusively of corporate presidents in six cities. I followed in some pretty big footsteps: others who had addressed these clubs included media mogul Ted Turner; Herb Kelleher, CEO of Southwest Airlines; Mo Siegel, founder of Celestial Seasonings Tea; and "Famous Amos," the cookie king.

The invitation came out of the blue. Still, it was not an accident. The man in charge of these clubs had been on my mailing list for years. All the cumulative publicity I'd obtained, the books I'd written and had published, other groups I'd spoken for, praise from other business leaders, my very active profile in several associations added up to an impact that led to this important invitation. I didn't directly ask for this particular speaking opportunity; so in that sense, you could call this a happy accident. But when you understand how very deliberate positioning made it possible, you'd call it anything but accidental.

A Story of Positioning Success

The story of Roger M., who skyrocketed from $5,000.00 to $50,000.00 a month in commissions, illustrates how important positioning can be. Roger had been in the business of selling franchises and business opportunities for nearly ten years, making a very good living, averaging about $5,000.00 a month in commissions, when he hit on the idea that "selling" was the wrong positioning. By pursuing people, he was chasing them away. He was on the defensive too much.

Roger has developed a strategy since copied by many in his industry. Early in the process of conversing with and providing information to prospective franchisees, Roger requires them to provide two business or professional references and two personal references. Then, he calls those references and asks them questions, ostensibly to determine the character, integrity, and other general qualifications of the person. He tells these references that he is considering this person as well as several others for the purpose of granting one of them a very valuable arrangement with his corporation. Well, what do you think happens right after those calls take place?

Right. Those four people immediately call his prospect to tell them they were called and to regurgitate their conversations. The prospect now feels that he is competing and qualifying for the opportunity, not being "sold" the opportunity.

Roger switched his positioning from *selling* to *selecting*. In the first year with his new strategy, Roger's income jumped from $60,000.00 to more than $500,000.00.

What does this have to do with your shoe store, restaurant, insurance agency, or widget distribution business? Everything! Roger's "trick" shows the income-multiplying power of positioning.

I have written about this at greater length, and provided more examples, in the companion book to this one, *No B.S. Sales Success.*

Who Do You Think You Are?

There's an old story that many speakers have appropriated and told as their own.

The featured guest speaker seated at the head table says to the waiter, "Bring me some more butter." The waiter says, "Can't. One pat of butter per person." "Do you know who I am?" asks the frustrated speaker. "Nope," says the waiter. "Who are you?"

"I am a famous author, here tonight as the featured guest speaker. After dinner, I'm going to share my wisdom with all these people. This group has brought me in at great expense. That's who I am. And I want another pat of butter."

"Well," says the waiter, "do you know who I am?"

"No," admits the speaker.

The waiter smiles triumphantly. "I am the man in charge of the butter."

The point of the story is that we all need to maintain some modesty and some appreciation for everybody else's right to be important. But in positioning yourself and your business for success, you have to clearly determine who you are, then drive that message home to your marketplace. And it's important to make the right decision. The marketplace will usually accept the positioning you choose for yourself and present to others. You really are in control.

CHAPTER 5

How Entrepreneurs *Really*
Make Money—*Big* Money!

Humorous writer Robert Benchley admitted that, after 15 years,
he had concluded he had no real talent for writing.
"But then it was too late," he said. "I can't quit
because I'm too famous."

aul Hawken, the extraordinarily insightful expert on the
entrepreneurial experience, wrote in his book *Growing a
Business*, "The more exposure I gained to the 'official' world
of business, the more I began to doubt that I was in business
at all. I seemed to be doing something entirely different. I get that
same feeling today when I read most of the standard literature."

When I read that, I said, "Me too!" And I suspect that many
readers of this book may feel that way because I'm writing for the
entrepreneur more than I am the small-business owner. Although
they can be the same, they are usually very different.

The typical small-business owner marries a specific, nar-
rowly defined business, manages it, and, essentially, employs

himself or herself as a general manager. When you start a business, buy a business, or buy a franchise, you really buy yourself a job, hopefully a very good job. You make money by taking a salary, benefits, and perks. In the long term, you may make a significant sum that you can retire on when you sell your business. If you get rich, it will probably be by stabilizing your first store, then opening a second, then a third, and eventually developing a chain. Your first business may only give you $30,000.00, $35,000.00, or $40,000.00 a year in income—the equivalent of a good job. Six such businesses, though, may give you $180,000.00 to $240,000.00 a year and allow you to become quietly, slowly rich.

There's nothing wrong with this model. In fact, there's a lot that's right about it. There are a lot of millionaires made slowly by very "ordinary" small businesses. According to Thomas Stanley, professor of marketing at Georgia State University, a serious student of the affluent in America, and author of the bestseller *The Millionaire Next Door*, most millionaires make their money "the old-fashioned ways: hard work for thirty years, six days a week . . . in businesses that cater to the needs of ordinary people." His and other research shows that a lot of owners of small businesses get rich slowly and steadily over 30, 40, or even 50 years. This serves to demonstrate that you certainly don't need a revolutionary new mousetrap to get rich; there are still plenty of unexploited opportunities in already established, proven fields of business, and you can build wealth in any number of these fields just by doing things a hair better than the average.

But *true* entrepreneurs do things a little differently, and looking carefully at how they really make money should open your eyes to new and different opportunities, too.

What Are You Going to Do When You Grow Up?

The true entrepreneur is *not* married to a specific business. If you ask the typical small-business owner what he or she does, you'll get a narrow, easily understood answer: I own a restaurant. I'm a jeweler. I own a gift shop. The entrepreneur's answer is never that simple. I imagine both my parents died still wondering exactly what I was going to be when I grew up. My father died when I was 48.

Entrepreneurs, first and foremost, make their money with innovative *ideas.* They are creators much more than they are managers. For this reason, they often start, develop, and sell a business only to move on and do it all over again. Some entrepreneurs who try to stay get forced out by their investors, who correctly recognize that being very talented at creating businesses does not necessarily mean that you are talented in managing a maturing business.

Usually, entrepreneurs are in many businesses, not one, even when it looks like one. This is the case with my clients and friends Bill Guthy and Greg Renker. Guthy's initial business was an audiocassette duplicating business for speakers and conventions. Then he got interested in using his production capability for proprietary products he could market, not just as a contract manufacturer for others; that led to a licensing agreement with the Napoleon Hill Foundation for an audio product based on the book *Think and Grow Rich.* Next, as Bill saw several of the people he was duplicating cassettes for doing well with television infomercials, he decided to produce a TV show to sell *Think and Grow Rich* tapes.

Today, the Guthy-Renker Corporation is a $600-million-a-year leader in the infomercial field and might be defined as an infomercial production company. But under the umbrella is another collection of diverse businesses. For example, behind their "Personal Power" TV programs with Tony Robbins is an entire publishing business, a cassette-a-month club business, and mailing-list business; behind their Victoria Principal skin-care program is a mail-order cosmetics business. Over the years, the business has changed from being "next hit" infomercial driven to being an umbrella company over vertical businesses that are continuity driven. These currently include Pro-Activ acne treatment products, Victoria Principal skin care, Susan Lucci skin care, and Comprehensive Nutrition—each with its own clientele receiving automatic shipments of product every 30 or 60 days.

There's no simple answer to "what do you do?" for Bill and Greg. And, they are in eager search of their next great idea, their next new business within their business. The money made managing the business is mostly made for them by other, hired managers. They make their money with ideas.

Another of my clients, Craig Proctor, is a real estate agent entrepreneur, which makes him very different from 90,000 other agents he outperforms every year.

For starters, as a real estate agent (not a broker) Craig handles over $100 million a year of residential real estate transactions, but he does so part-time. He has a second, large, thriving business— or, more accurately, group of businesses—selling his business methods, ads, Web sites, and such to other agents, conducting two giant seminars a year for agents, and providing tele-coaching to 400 or so agents every month. In order to fit it all into a 40-hour workweek, he looks for leverage every place he can get it. He is a heavy user of what we call "marketing technologies"— for example, driving his prospective home sellers or buyers to prerecorded 800-number "hotlines" or Web sites and mailing them information before investing time talking to them. He also employs other agents to show homes to his buyers and do listing presentations for him to sellers. Consequently, he handles about 2,000 advertising and referral-generated leads per month, more than a typical agent handles in two years.

While most real estate agents view themselves as real estate agents, Craig views himself as an entrepreneur in the real estate field. It is far more than a semantic difference.

The Fortune-Building Secret of Total Customer Value

I am amazed at business owners who do not have mailing lists of their customers. I am amazed at the businesses that never do anything when they lose customers. And I am amazed at the businesses that do nothing to maximize their Total Customer Value—TCV.

The customer who is satisfied with you and trusts you is an enormous, enormously exploitable asset. Let's say you have a neighborhood dry cleaning business. Most dry cleaners take whatever business comes their way, live on their repeat business, and never think much more about it. But let's think about the entrepreneurial dry cleaner who understands TCV. Here are some of the things you'll see that dry cleaner doing:

- *Aggressively expanding usage of core services by repeat customers.* With in-store displays, bag stuffers, handouts, coupons, and mailings, the entrepreneurial dry cleaner encourages customers to use leather and suede cleaning services, spot removal, fur storage, necktie cleaning, etc. By continually reminding these customers of all the different services offered, the total purchase average per customer per year will increase. If the dry cleaner increases the total purchases of a customer by just $4.00 per month— or $48.00 per year—and keeps that customer for 10 years, that's a $480.00 swing in the plus direction. With just 500 customers, that's $240,000.00, and if the dry cleaner does that to four outlets, that's a creation of an extra $1 million!

- *Diversifying into joint ventures or "hosting" other businesses with some logical relationship to his or her own.* The dry cleaner rearranges the location's layout to free up a corner for a shoe repair shop and arranges with a local shoe repair shop owner for the repair person to be on premises two afternoons a week. The rest of the time, repair work is dropped off at the cleaners one day, back and ready for the customers the next. Of course, the shoe repair corner also stocks and sells quality lines of shoe polishes, brushes, laces, etc. The dry cleaner and two friends get in the carpet and drapery cleaning business and promote that business to the dry-cleaning customers. Several times a year (e.g., Christmas, Father's Day, etc.), the dry cleaner brings in displays of high-quality men's neckties and offers them at very good prices, as "impulse buys" to customers.

- *Exploiting the testimonial and referral potential of the customer list.* Using a criss-cross street directory, the dry cleaner builds a list of all the people who live next door to or across the street from satisfied customers. Then, on a Saturday, using a small army of staff and neighborhood kids, he goes out and personally calls on these prospects, letting them know that their neighbors are customers, inviting them to try the services, and giving out coupons. Follow-up is accomplished by using a series of postcards sent through the mail. With such a targeted, personalized approach, a large number of new customers are added to the base with nominal expense. This is a very different way of thinking about business.

> While most business owners think that the purpose of getting a customer is to make a sale, my clients and I do the reverse; we make a sale to get a customer.

When I go out on a speaking engagement or to conduct a seminar, I'm viewed as a professional speaker, and I'm paid a substantial fee for my services as a speaker ($8,300.00, as of this writing). But I'm a very entrepreneurial speaker. When I'm speaking, I'm also acquiring customers with great, long-term potential value. First of all, at every speech, I'll offer and sell appropriate, relevant books, cassettes, and home-study courses. Second, those buyers will subsequently get our catalogues, one of our newsletters, and a series of offers by direct mail to create additional purchases. Third, they'll be sold a subscription to one of our newsletters or a tape-a-month program or both. Fourth, they'll be encouraged to attend other, future seminars. Fifth, in many cases, they'll become prospects for our direct-marketing conferences, my consulting services, or my direct-response copy-writing services. My publishing/mail-order company has many customers who buy from us several times a year, year after year after year, who were acquired by my giving a speech 5, 8, 10, even 20 years ago.

The details in the above paragraph no longer apply in the way they did when I first wrote this book and that example, but the concept has not changed. Today I no longer own and operate my product/publishing business or my newsletter business. But I do receive royalty income from them, and I do funnel customers to them. Today I have a coaching business I did not have then, and speaking funnels customers to coaching as well.

The point is, I'm thinking of the customer as a very important asset with continuous, expandable lifetime value. There are customers who have given me income as recently as this month who were acquired when they first saw me speak 20 years ago. I know, because I track every one of them.

If you are to be a successful entrepreneur, it's important to think in terms of VALUE, not just sales or profits, and to think in terms of long-term and total value, not just immediate value.

Looking for Value in All the Wrong Places

I would never buy—or let a client buy—a business without a good list of its customers' names, addresses, fax numbers, e-mail addresses, and telephone numbers. Nor should you.

Most business owners mistakenly place high value on the physicality of business: storefront, office, factory, equipment, inventory. But all that is easily replaceable and duplicatable. It's just "stuff."

All the real value is in the customers.

This is why the smartest, richest entrepreneurs I know make sure they never involve themselves in anything where they don't have direct access to and a direct relationship with the end-user customers. For those of us who understand the incomparable value of controlling the relationship with the customer, it's always painful to be in any other situation. My friend Jeff Paul recently developed a product, a financial organizer kit, to be sold on home shopping TV. He sold more than 165,000 units on QVC but because of QVC's contract requirements, Jeff got no access to the customers and could not even put his business identity into the product so they might find him. Yes, Jeff made quite a bit of money from these sales—but only once. Zap, done, over. He knows how to develop customers into repeat customers, so he conservatively estimates the money he *won't* make because he can't get to these customers to exceed the money he did make by 500%. As I said, painful.

Let me give you just one example of how important "the list" is, in an ordinary, mundane business: a restaurant. Fewer than 5% of all independently owned restaurants have a database of their customers. My client and Platinum Member Rory Fatt of Restaurant Marketing Systems has a relatively simple system for conducting birthday promotions to restaurants' customers. This automatically provides 12 promotions a year, because there are birthdays every month. Last year, one of his "star" clients, the owner of four restaurants, tracked more than $400,000.00 in sales directly to his birthday promotion e-mails.

"Wait just a minute," says the skeptic, " he'd have gotten a lot of that business anyway from those regular customers."

Maybe yes, maybe no. But think about this: no one celebrates their birthday in a restaurant alone. They come in pairs and groups. They introduce new customers to the restaurant for the first time, who get added to the list, who get their own birthday offer, who then bring more first-time customers, who then get added to the list.

This simple strategy isn't limited to restaurants. It is only limited to business owners with good lists, and the foresight to collect customers' birth months as added data.

Networking and Joint Ventures

Today's successful, innovative entrepreneur is very much in tune with the idea of cooperative marketing and with networking with other entrepreneurs for mutual benefit and profit.

A member of one of my coaching groups, Bob Higgins, owner of Higgins Painting, often does cross-promotional joint ventures with another of my members in his town, T. A. Schmitt, who owns a photography studio. What does a house painting company and a photography studio have in common? Well, not much. But enough. They each have customers who spend money and were originated with smart direct marketing. So Bob includes free gifts and coupons from Schmitt in his offers; Schmitt gives away Bob's coupons to his customers. Together, they organized a local group of other merchants, who all share costs of joint direct-mail campaigns. And so on.

My client Joe Polish teaches the owners of carpet cleaning businesses to seek out similar joint venture relationships with dry cleaners, carpet stores, furniture stores, pest control operators, even real estate agents. If a cleaner has ten such arrangements, each only minimally productive, each producing only one new customer a month, that's 120 new customers a year with zero or near-zero acquisition cost. The customer has a five-year value of more than $2,000.00, so that's $240,000.00. Nothing to sneeze at.

In Phoenix, there are hundreds of restaurants. But one restaurant owner also has his own TV cooking show; markets videocassettes, cookbooks, classes, and seminars; arranges murder mystery nights at his restaurant promoted in joint venture with a theater group; runs a catering business; and hosts a "culinary capitals of the world" cruise twice a year.

His cooperative relationship with the travel agency for arranging the cruise is an excellent example of a successful joint venture. The travel agency packages the cruise for him to sell to his clients; it also offers it to their customers and promotes his restaurant to its customers. In turn, he promotes the travel agency to his customers. Each has nurtured its valuable customer lists. By letting each other tap those customer lists, both benefit, and both further enhance their Total Customer Value.

The Remarkable Value of a Duplicative Model

My friend and former client Len Shykind had a collection of a few dozen different business cards framed, hanging on his office wall. All the cards were his own from the various businesses he had struggled with prior to hitting his home run with Gold By The Inch. Len invented the idea of taking gold jewelry chain on the spools to high-traffic locations like swap meets and making bracelets to size, on the spot, for customers, rather than displaying and selling pre-sized bracelets. The public loved this concept. Whenever he set up his display, people flocked around—and bought jewelry.

Len was smart enough to realize he'd invented a business that just about anybody could do. He had a duplicative model.

He quickly recruited tens of thousands of Gold By The Inch distributors throughout the United States, Canada, and elsewhere—some full-time, most part time. They began setting up their portable businesses at swap meets, in bazaars, in stores, and in kiosks. Together they sold tens of millions of dollars worth of Gold By The Inch every year. In fact, the market was so big and the need for more distributors so great, I produced a TV infomercial for Len to interest people in getting into this business. That program ran on national cable networks for eight years and made Len so wealthy that he was able to take a very early retirement.

Tom Monahan turned a single pizza joint into the Domino's empire with a duplicative model for a pizza delivery business. Fred DeLuca created a model for a sub sandwich shop with a unique factor: fresh-baked rolls, no grill requiring vents, and a simple operations plan. Today, Subway nips at the heels of the giant with the golden arches!

As you drive down the street and see fast-food franchises, instant printing franchises, and dry-cleaning stores, you're seeing the power of duplicative models at work. If you attend a Tupperware party, buy an Amway product, stop in an airport for a TCBY yogurt cone, or have a Dura-Clean carpet cleaner come to your home, you're seeing the power of a duplicative model at work. Even without the complexities of creating franchises or distributorships, the duplicative approach makes many entrepreneurs wealthy.

One way or another, the astute entrepreneur works at reducing the driving forces of his business to replicatable systems so his business can run profitably without him and then often finds ways

I have helped more than 80 different individuals with successful businesses built on duplicative models become "gurus" to their respective industries, package up what they do and sell it—or, in some cases, license it—to others in their fields, and develop lucrative coaching businesses in their industries.

For example, Craig Proctor, the real estate agent I mentioned earlier, has 400 or so real estate agents, each paying $800.00 a month to Craig for tele-coaching and the right to use Craig's ads as their own. Joe Polish, a once-broke carpet cleaner who turned around his cleaning business with an unusual marketing approach, has more than 3,000 other carpet cleaners paying to use his ads and marketing materials, and nearly 100 in his top-level coaching program, each paying $10,000.00 a year for the privilege. Comparables to Craig and Joe are Ron Ipach, in the auto repair industry; Rory Fatt, restaurants; Bill Hammond, lawyers; Chauncey Hutter, tax preparers and accountants; Marty Grunder, landscaping companies—a more complete list is included in my *Million Dollar Resource Directory* at www.dankennedy.com.

The point is, these 80+ companies are all based on my duplicatable model that lets a successful business leader package his experience in a given business and use it to extract a fortune from the rest of his industry.

NO B.S. **Business Success** 97

to leverage the work he's done in perfecting those systems for himself into yet another business: selling the systems to others.

Mastering the Six Entrepreneurial Competencies

Figure 5.1 illustrates the six competencies the entrepreneur must master. One big difference between a small business owner and an entrepreneur is the emphasis given each of these competencies and whether they are approached sequentially or simultaneously.

The business owner typically gives 70% of his attention to Competency #1, 20% to #2, 9% to #3, and 1% to #4. Ever so gradually, over time, if he gets smarter and if he's making money, the ratios shift. Late in the game, he tackles #5. He hardly ever thinks about #6. If he does, it's in context of retirement. The business owner is often comfortable only with #1, having gotten into business in the first place to *do* the thing, not to *market* it. A more accurate visual depiction of the business owner's relationship to these competencies would be #2 through #6 as small boxes inside one big box identified as "The Business," with #1 as its function.

For the entrepreneur, the six competencies illustration is an "overlay" for any business, moved from one business to another. He feels he can move his attention fluidly from one box to another as warranted.

While the business owner may work to implement these competencies inside a particular business, the entrepreneur works to master these competencies, *period*. (See Figure 5.2.)

Live Outside the Lines

If given a shoe store, the small-business owner will manage and promote that shoe store well. But ten years from now, it will still

CHAPTER 5 / HOW ENTREPRENEURS *REALLY* MAKE MONEY—*BIG* MONEY!

be a shoe store. Give that same shoe store to a true entrepreneur, and ten years from now, you probably won't recognize it!

Maybe, as a child, you were urged to "color inside the lines." This was not great training for entrepreneurial success! As you can see, most entrepreneurs make most of their money "outside the lines."

FIGURE 5.1: Core Entrepreneurial Competencies

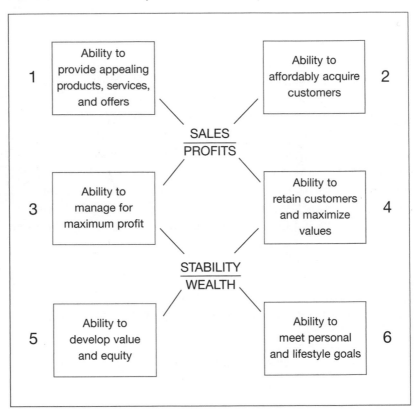

FIGURE **5.2:** Portable Entrepreneurial Overlay

	1		2		3		4		5		6	
	Ability to provide appealing prod-ucts, services, and offers		Ability to affordably acquire customers		Ability to manage for maximum profit		Ability to retain customers and maximize values		Ability to develop value and equity		Ability to meet personal and lifestyle goals	
	Strengths	Need to Improve	Strengths	Need to Improve	Strengths	Need to Improve	Strengths	Need to Improve	Strengths	Need to Improve	Strengths	Need to Improve

CHAPTER 6

How to Create Exciting Sales and Marketing Breakthroughs

People love to buy.

—Bill Gove

O K, here it is—what you probably bought this book for: a no holds barred, no B.S. collection of breakthrough strategies to get rich, preferably quick.

By the way, nothing wrong with quick and no special virtue in slow. I know you've been told that "get rich quick schemes" are bad news. But the word *scheme* has simply been tarred with a broad black brush. A good, sound scheme is a perfectly fine thing. And when you deposit money at the bank, you don't get penalized for having made it quickly or easily.

And contrary to popular myth, a lot of fortunes *are* made fast.

Once Dave Thomas got really cooking, pardon the pun, he opened 1,000 Wendy's restaurants in one year.

I've been very fortunate to work with quite a few people who've made a point of getting rich quick. Bob Scheinfeld, for example, took a company from $1.3 million to $44 million in sales in just four years, then sold it for $177 million the fifth year. Referring back to our earlier discussion about "value," incidentally, notice he increased sales 44 times but increased value nearly 177 times. One of my coaching clients, Steve Clauson took his company from $2 million to $25 million in three years. My students Jeff Paul and Matt Furey both took their mail-order type businesses from zero to $100,000.00 a month in under a year. I have routinely increased established companies' profits 200% to 500% in a single year.

These kind of gigantic, fast leaps come from only one place: sales and marketing breakthroughs.

The big money in the world is made in sales and marketing. Nobody gets rich dusting shelves, changing light bulbs, keeping books, or managing employees. Yet I'm amazed at how many entrepreneurs let such things suck up all their time, focused on everything and anything but sales and marketing.

So let's get this straight from the start: the place for you to direct your time, energy, creativity, common sense, hard work, and resources is marketing.

> In fact, the first quantum leap from ordinary good-job-type income to big entrepreneur-type income occurs very rapidly after the business owner makes the intellectual, emotional, and actual switch from "doer" of his "thing" to "marketer" of his "thing."

The fact that marketing's where the money is can be seen in small or big businesses.

Some years ago, I was doing a lot of consulting and advertising copywriting work for a big company owned by an even bigger *Fortune* 500 company. Its president, a nice, pleasant fellow, called me in to his private office, closed the door, sat across from me and said, "I've done some calculations and realized we are actually paying you more per hour than we are paying me."

Imagine being a consultant confronted with this one!

I answered, "There is a very good reason for that. You see, you know how to do everything in this company better than I do by a big margin except for one thing, and it is essential and vital that one thing gets done the best way it can, because nothing you know how to do matters if it doesn't. That one thing is getting customers. That's the one thing I know how to do that you don't, and that's why I get paid more. But look, " I said, "we'll just keep this as our private secret."

That is a true story, and it makes more than one important point. One is, as I've said, that any rapid and dramatic value improvement in a business is going to come from the sales and marketing side, and usually the only indispensably valuable people are the ones who know how to create sales and marketing breakthroughs. Two, you do not want to be in the position of that corporate CEO. You do not want a guy like me holding you and your success hostage. The only way to prevent that is to personally master the sales and marketing aspects of your business.

At Least Avoid the Ultimate Marketing Sin

The worst marketing sin you can commit is to be boring. People love to buy when it's a pleasure to buy.

I've created more marketing breakthroughs by being exciting, different, and outrageous than by any other means. Many have emulated me.

Bill Glazer, my Platinum Member and the publisher of my *No B.S. Marketing Letter,* is known nationally for the "Outrageous Advertising" he creates for his own wildly successful menswear stores and provides to other store owners nationwide. He has sent out direct-mail pieces that look like hand-scrawled notes on a diner's placemat, complete with coffee cup stains; handwritten notes on torn legal pad paper; and notes on lunch bags. He utilizes incredible guarantees.

Dr. Gregg Nielsen, a long-time Member who has been studying me for 20 years, does the most outrageous advertising and marketing in the entire chiropractic profession. Figure 6.1 is a copy of one of his direct-mail pieces, a funny letter from his staff. I've included it so you can get a feel for what I'm talking about. Believe me, his doctor peers and even his wife cringe at mailings like this. But his patients love it and refer like crazy—at a rate five times better than his profession's average.

I could show you hundreds more examples from the ever-growing tribe of like-minded marketers I've inspired.

Their output is the antithesis of dull, boring, institutional, stuffy professional marketing.

Another of the marketing wizards I've inspired, Pamela Yellen, CEO of Prospecting and Marketing Institute, has financial advisors very successfully obtaining appointments with high-ranking corporate executives who have at least several million dollars of personal, investable assets by sending them a full-sized canoe paddle in the mail. The accompanying letter begins "If your current investment advisors have left you up the river without a paddle . . . ."

Boring is boring. Leap-out-at-you, outrageous, fun, and interesting is what it is. People are people, in the boardroom on the 50th floor or on the floor in the living room.

The entrepreneur's responsibility and opportunity is to create breakthrough ideas that foster exciting, positive relationships between the company and its customers. This chapter gives you the very best ways I know to create those kinds of breakthrough ideas.

Breakthrough Strategy #1: Find a Niche Market and Exploit It

In niches, there are riches!

A market niche is a crack, a crevice, an opportunity gap, sometimes a tiny segment of a market being overlooked, ignored, abused, or very poorly serviced.

I know of a printing company specializing in medical forms for hospitals. It (and its competitors) packaged and sold their various forms in cartons of 1,000, 5,000, and 10,000. Many small hospitals and nursing homes refused to buy from them because they didn't need 1,000 copies of any one form. The president of this printing company took the time to ask how many forms they would buy. He then put out a new catalogue with all the forms priced in packages of 150 for smaller hospitals and institutions, and in short order, it captured the niche market of small institutions.

When I spoke at the national convention of the Floor Coverings International company, I saw another good example. This company recognized that although most people can't afford an interior designer when they buy new carpeting for their homes, most of them also lack confidence in choosing the right color, style, and texture to suit their particular needs. People find

In 1983, I was doing some speaking for a practice management company in the chiropractic profession and another in the dental profession. As I analyzed the professions, I identified an enormous "gap" in what was being offered to help doctors market, promote, and grow their practices. There were a number of management companies offering multiyear programs requiring fees upwards from $30,000.00 per doctor. There were books and how-to manuals in the trade journals for $10.00 to $50.00. But there was nothing in between.

It also was true that almost all the management companies acquired their clients by inviting doctors to free seminars, then delivering sales presentations, ultimately asking for $30,000.00 or more.

I devised a company that would copycat the entire seminar method but offer do-it-yourself-type "marketing kits" and complete courses for $400.00 to $1,000.00.

We hit the "price gap" perfectly. Within the first 12 months, the company I created became THE largest seminar and publishing company exclusively serving chiropractors and dentists. Actually, we became that our first day because we were the *only* company mixing chiropractors and dentists into the same seminars; I defined my own niche, so I could trumpet being the biggest instantly. Beyond that, we did quickly grow to millions of dollars. We trained well over 10,000 doctors.

it hard to pick the right carpet in a store, away from their own walls, furniture, and environment. So Floor Coverings International equipped its franchisees with "mobile" stores in vans that go to customers' houses; they provide samples and swatches of different carpets for consideration without the high-priced interior decorator.

My coaching client B. Shawn Warren has a hugely profitable business virtually invisible to anyone not in leadership in a fraternal organization—like the Shriners or Kiwanis—but those folks know him well because he is the dominant provider of awards, promotional items, glassware, apparel, and other products emblazoned with these organizations' logos. He also publishes a newsletter about group leadership for the clients who buy these goods from him. Almost all the merchandise his company sells can be provided by any of the thousands of "generic" ad specialty companies, but Shawn has created a niche business and dominated a target market.

Breakthrough Strategy #2: Find a New Sales Medium and Let It Make You Rich

In Arizona, there is an industrial cleaning products manufacturer with a very successful line of citrus-peel-based cleaners and stain removers. For years, they bottled these chemicals in giant drums and sold them to factories, restaurants, hospitals, hotels, and other large institutional buyers. Like every other industrial chemical company, the only sales media they used were industrial sales representatives and catalogs distributed to their customers.

They made the leap to marketing directly to consumers through a new sales medium—a shopping channel on cable TV. It works for them because their products demonstrate like magic tricks. They're perfect for television. After their first on-the-air test, they couldn't bottle product fast enough. They are "TV best-sellers," and this very different sales media has made these entrepreneurs rich, quick.

The late Bill McGowan, the crusty visionary who put MCI on the map, proved the value of exploring new sales media. He had the daring to market long-distance telephone services via, of all things, multilevel marketing! Through a strategic alliance between MCI and Amway, Amway distributors sold MCI services right along with their own products and subsequently brought hundreds of thousands of new MCI customers on board at a rapid-fire pace. MCI's daring decision to use a controversial, often-criticized sales medium and to form this unusual marriage made it millions of dollars. Another entrepreneur who created a multilevel company selling telephone services, Excel Communications, made the 2003 *Forbes* List of America's 400 richest people.

The Internet has provided a whole new arena of opportunity, via two media channels, Web sites and e-mail.

This is not the "magic bean" it has been made out to be, and its wide open, unregulated frontier-like atmosphere is changing rapidly. However, for many entrepreneurs, it has been a source of real sales breakthroughs.

I consulted with an importer of very expensive, artisan-created, one-of-a-kind iron beds from Argentina. Guys reading this might not know—but women do—this is a romantic product. Anyway, due to the one-of-a-kind nature of each bed and the prices, he'd been unable to make any headway with traditional distribution channels, such as furniture stores or catalogs. But with tiny ads in certain magazines, he was able to attract customers to his own Web site and sell these beds for $3,000.00 to $10,000.00 each, direct to individuals. Because a Web site offers endless display space fundamentally at no cost, he could display as many individual designs as he liked.

My Platinum Member Matt Furey went from zero to more than $100,000.00 a month in income from his homebased business selling his self-published *Combat Conditioning* book and other publications of interest to martial arts and fitness buffs—all via the Internet. He's gone on to develop a more diverse, multiproduct business using offline marketing such as magazine ads and direct mail as well as online, generating millions of dollars annually. Now Matt also has a very profitable second business, teaching his methods for creating profitable direct marketing to others. He is also the exclusive, master licensee from the Psycho-Cybernetics Foundation, of which I am CEO, and he handles all the distribution of all the Psycho-Cybernetics books, cassettes, and materials. All this because he mastered use of a new marketing media.

You'll find more about the Internet in Chapter 18.

Internet aside, many sales breakthroughs don't require a new media becoming available; instead they come from fitting a product together with an existing media not previously used for that type of product.

My friend Joe Sugarman, a bona fide direct-marketing legend, has had mammoth success with his product Blu-Blockers sunglasses. Today, you can buy them in retail stores and in catalogs, but their launch was via a 30-minute TV infomercial. That success in turn led to QVC, the home shopping channel, where millions of pairs have been sold. To my knowledge, sunglasses had never been sold via infomercial before Joe.

Recently, doctors have promoted Botox injections via Tupperware-style party plan selling. The in-home sales party's certainly not a new media. But doctors using it, that's new.

Breakthrough Strategy #3: Create a New Type of Guarantee and Confound Your Competition

I love marketing on the strength of guarantees. For me, nothing's better than finding a way to offer the very best guarantee in any given field.

I've been told that guarantees are outdated, overdone, and no longer effective, but my experience proves this to be non-sense. Good guarantees work just as well today as they did 25 years ago, and they may be more necessary than ever.

Lee Iacocca used this idea to save Chrysler years back, with its seven-year/70,000 mile warranty along with the argument: if you want to know who builds them better, take a look at who guarantees them longer. At the time, this was a ground-breaking guarantee. It left the competition gasping and galloping back-wards. It got the public's attention, and it sold a lot of cars. (Eventually, of course, the competition caught up. That's to be expected.)

About 30 years ago, my ad agency had a small chain of eye-glass stores as a client, and we created, I believe before anyone else in the country, the "free eyeglass replacement guarantee." My client ran large newspaper ads featuring this remarkable guarantee—and he brought in a flood of customers. He sucked customers right out of his competitors' stores. His stores kicked butt for nearly a year with this promotion. In one store, sales increased by 800%. Today, big chains, such as Pearle Vision Centers, use the same strategy.

Many of the audiocassette courses and business-building systems that I sell from the speaker's platform, I sell with a guar-antee, but not the typical 30-, 60-, or 90-day guarantee—instead a full 12-month guarantee. I say, "Use the advice for up to 12 months, and if not thrilled and eager to get more, send back the

books and tapes for a full refund." In one instance, with one program, I guarantee that you, the buyer, will make at least
$25,000.00 in 12 months by following its guidance or you can get
your money back. Some of my high-priced seminars have been
sold with as much as double-your-money-back guarantees.

I know of no other professional speaker who offers the kind
of strong, clear, straightforward guarantees that I do. In fact, I say
that if most people had to guarantee what comes out of their
mouths, they'd go mute in a heartbeat or broke in a New York
minute. These guarantees give me immense power and my customers great confidence.

I have clients who use what we call "penalty guarantees."
Financial advisors who guarantee they will uncover and present
hidden opportunities to a new client in the first one hour meeting or pay the client $100.00 to $1,000.00 for wasting his time.
Marketers who guarantee reading their lengthy sales letters will
be worthwhile or the reader can say his time was wasted and be
paid $25.00, $50.00, or $100.00. An appliance company that guar-
antees service on time or they do the repair work free.

You should also think about the way you describe and present your guarantees. My client Guthy-Renker Corporation has
had Victoria Principal delivering her bottom-of-the-jar guarantee:
use the whole jar, return it empty, if dissatisfied, for refund. Still
the best worded guarantee in skin care that I've ever seen came
from my friend, copywriting genius Gary Halbert, for Nancy
Kwan's Pearl Cream: "If your friends don't actually accuse you of
having had a face-lift, return the empty jar . . . ." I swiped it for a
weight-loss product: "If your friends don't accuse you of having
had liposuction . . . ." These are nothing more than ordinary satisfaction guarantees presented in more interesting ways.

It may be marketing consultant Jay Abraham who coined the term "risk reversal selling" for the use of strong, creatively worded guarantees. Whether he originated it or not, he and I share the position of being committed advocates of risk reversal. Every time I have convinced a client to take a particularly daring risk reversal position, his increased sales have far exceeded the cost of honoring the guarantees.

Breakthrough Strategy #4: Deliver Exceptional Service and Earn Word-of-Mouth Advertising

As a customer these days, aren't you frustrated more often than not? I find spending money as tough as making it! Think about all the aggravations you have had as a customer and the number of times you've turned away from a business because of poor service.

What is exceptional service? It means different things to different people in different businesses at different times, so I can't define it for you in your business with a general statement. But I can tell you where to look and who to study to get close to it.

Walt Disney preached that customers should be viewed and treated like guests. That's why at Disney World and Disneyland all the employees, from the broom pushers to the managers, learn how to direct guests to any attraction and how to answer the most common questions. They are taught that they are important to the success of each guest's visit. The next time you're at a Disney park, stand near a broom pusher for a few minutes. Watch how people go up and ask questions. Watch how well that employee responds. You'll witness exceptional customer service in action.

My favorite Disney marketing principle is *do what you do so well that people can't resist telling others about you.* Following this principle gives you marketing leverage. A lot of leverage. If you get one customer from an advertisement, that's one thing, but if you get that customer plus three referrals, who in turn refer two people, that's nine new customers from leverage rather than direct monetary investment.

As service overall worsens, your opportunity to stand out through service increases.

Breakthrough Strategy #5: Seek Strategic Marketing Alliances

I am about to give you the most powerful secret to extracting outrageous profits from just about any business, so pay attention. There is one marketing guru who charges (and gets) $15,000.00 per person to teach this single secret to entrepreneurs—and when they have heard him, they cheerfully pay and leave happy.

The secret I reveal is the only known antidote to the biggest, nagging problem of all business, that is, the difficulty and very high costs of acquiring new customers.

You may or may not know it, but most businesses lose money on their first sales to new customers. In effect, they "buy" their customers with the hope of profit from subsequent sales. They make an investment in getting their customers, and there is nothing wrong with that.

Certainly, you can build a successful business losing money on every first sale. It's done every day by restaurants, retail stores, and mail-order companies. I do it, too. But I sure don't like it. Any time I can eliminate that cost out of the business formula, I get very excited. You will too, when you understand that the fastest, most profitable thing you can ever do in business is to "steal" someone else's customers rather than investing your own money in ferreting out customers from scratch.

So how is this done?

Thomas G. is an expert in buying foreclosure real estate at enormous discounts, and he wrote a very thorough, very professional, very pricey book about it. He then went to another fellow, who published a newsletter on financial matters, investing, taxes, business opportunities, and so on, for 5,000 subscribers. This newsletter publisher had invested a huge amount of money digging up these 5,000 people. He had run ads in magazines, sent direct-mail pieces, and paid for a toll-free number and a staff to take customer calls.

Thomas G. could have taken the same steps to find the same 5,000 people, but instead he struck a deal with the publisher. He provides 5,000 brochures and order forms for his books to be sent out with the next newsletter and offers to split the profits 50–50. Because the publisher likes Thomas G. and his product and he recognizes that he has a ready market for the product, he agrees. This is the basis for a strategic marketing alliance. One party has the customers; the other party has something "hot" to be sold to those customers. Simple. Sensible.

Thomas G. and his publisher "partner" sold 800 books. Thomas made $24,000.00 for minimal cost, and he also got 800 new customers for free. He is now in a position to sell other products directly to those people.

Can you apply this to any businesses? Sure you can. Consider the experience of the entrepreneur who opened a little deli and sandwich shop in a less-than-perfect location. He needed to get the word out, so he went to the nearby Exxon gas station, on a very busy corner, in a hot location, and asked them to hand out coupon books to their customers, display a poster advertising the deli, and place plastic sub sandwiches on top of the gas pumps. In return, the deli owner offered the manager and crew one free lunch for every ten coupons returned. In addition, he offered to distribute the gas station's own "winterize your car" coupons to his deli customers. Over a three-week period, the deli greeted more than 200 new customers.

One good way to ethically hijack someone else's customers that you judge ideally qualified to be your customers is to give that merchant something free, to give as gift or a premium to his customers. It will usually cost you less to "buy" ideal new customers this way than to get them through advertising. In my own business, I've let many publishers, speakers, and seminar companies give away $100-Value Coupons that I furnished, good for free, three-month trial subscriptions to my *No B.S. Marketing Letter,* and I've acquired lots of good subscriber-Members that way who've stayed with me for many years.

A lot of entrepreneurs fail to create the kind of strategic alliances and joint ventures that can provide a lot of good, new customers due to foolish reluctance to sufficiently give incentives and

---

Incidentally, a vitally important number to get a grip on in your business is: *what does it cost you to get a new customer?*

Another, *what will you pay to get a new customer?*

---

rewards to the source who can provide those customers, yet that same entrepreneur will cheerfully dump money into advertising.

Michael Kimble, CEO of Group-M Publishing, the company that publishes most of my information products, has obtained tens of thousands of customers through "parasite-ing" on other companies' mailing lists, customer lists, and inserts in their publications and packages. All these very productive relationships have been initiated by sending the likely candidates a letter boldly headlined: FREE MONEY. He offers the "host" what we call "free money" for letting him get his offer into their customer's hands; then he pays them generously for each sale made.

Breakthrough Strategy #6: Get Professional Prowess on a Percentage

I'm about to suggest hiring an expert or two to help you with your marketing. But, first, a few words about expert advice in general.

There are a lot of "experts" out there very eager to get their hands into your entrepreneurial pockets. Most of them aren't worth the powder it would take to blow them up. Most couldn't run your business or any other for a week. Most couldn't sell their way out of a closet. They may be good song 'n dance people, but that doesn't mean they can conceptualize a great song, write a musical, or attract crowds to the theater. When you peel away the top layer of veneer, you'll find another layer of veneer.

So, the expert advice I have for you about expert advice is to proceed with great caution. And I'm an expert!

Never let yourself be intimidated. Ask a lot of questions. Check references. Ultimately, trust your judgment and retain control. And, in the case of getting marketing assistance, get it from people willing, even eager, to be paid based on perform-ance, not on task completion.

You'll be hard-pressed to find a Madison Avenue ad agency that will play this way. If they did, they'd starve. The hard, tough truth is that most of what they do fails to work. It wins awards, it gets talked about, it jazzes up halftime at the Super Bowl, but it doesn't sell. That's why most agencies that win the industry's Clio Awards quickly lose the clients for which they created all that award-winning, expensive, but ineffective advertising. That's why in my seminars, when I've asked everybody to jot down the brand name of the battery advertised by the famous pink bunny banging his drum, one-third to one-half of all people write down the wrong brand name.

But every top marketing consultant and every top copy-writer I know eagerly looks for clients they can really help, then gets most of their compensation from a small percentage of the

Dan Kennedy's
Eternal Truth #8

No one will ever be a
bigger expert on your
business than you.

sales created and measured. For example, when I develop direct-marketing and direct-mail campaigns for a client, I charge a hefty fee, but as my main compensation, I take 2% to 5% of the resulting sales. My personal objective is to choose projects right and do the work so well that each client winds up paying me $50,000.00, $100,000.00, or more over time.

Also keep in mind that the best marketing experts do not tell you what to do. They try to create a partnership with you to combine your unique understanding of your business with their special expertise. Then they do the mechanics.

We realize no one's more of an expert on your business and your customers than you are, although you may benefit from help in extracting what you know and putting it into useable form.

A good marketing professional can save you a lot of time and trial-and-error experimentation, bring you already-proven ideas from their broader experience, and help you clarify your own thinking.

FIGURE **6.1:** Nielsen Exhibit

STAFF MEMO

FROM: Dr. Nielsen's Staff (Mostly Marie)
505 Aber Drive
Waterford, WI 53185
Ph: (262) 534-3767

Thursday 2:37 P.M.

"I Want To Give You A FREE Office Visit...Because... I'm Taking Full Responsibility For This Traffic Jam"

Dear Dan:

Hi again!!! As you can see, I've attached a little note to this letter. I'm doing this because I feel responsible for the traffic jam that happened in our office last Wednesday morning. And I want you to hear my side of the story first...before Dr. Nielsen tells you about it on your next office visit.

You see, last Wednesday morning our Yellow Pages ad representative stopped by to pick up our ad for the new Waterford phone book. He's a little old guy who always struts around in a cute, blue three-piece suit...and... he sports a white handlebar mustache. I think he looks like the guy from the Monopoly Game. And Wednesday morning he also finally decided to get treated for his headaches.

Anyway, Dr. Nielsen decided to change this year's Yellow Pages ad at the last minute. Mostly because Dr. Nielsen just added his FREE e-book, **"Wisconsin Fold Medicine"** (a collection of simple and easy home remedies) to his web site at www.doc nielsen.com... and... he also wanted to add this info to his new Yellow Pages ad just before the deadline Wednesday morning at noon.

Dr. Nielsen told me to have Stefi x-ray the ad rep, and throw out the old ad...because... he had a new ad. And he then gave the new ad to me to proofread. Maybe it was the full moon. Maybe it was all three phone lines ringing at the same time. Maybe it was all those people standing at the front desk staring at me. Maybe it was that 9 month old baby screaming nonstop while his mother jabbered on her cell phone in our lobby. And maybe it was just the combination of everything that day. Who knows?

In any event, I got slightly distracted. And I yelled to Stefi: *"Go ahead and x-ray the ad ...and... throw out the old rep."* You know, Stefi is so cool. She snagged Monopoly Man by the collar and muscled him out the front door. Then Stefi snatched Dr. Nielsen's new ad from me and x-rayed it. I've attached her x-ray of Dr. Nielsen's Yellow Pages ad as proof. For the record, she did a great job x-raying the ad.

Oh, the best part was when Dr. Nielsen asked Stefi why she was x-raying his Yellow Pages ad. I could not hear her response, because the lady with the cell phone was now standing in front of me yakking away...and her kid decided it was a good time to start screaming in my face. But, I bet Stefi's response was something like... *"I'm x-raying your Yellow Pages ad because it's my job, Sir."* Again, Stefi is so cool. She never questions anything around here. I guess that's a good thing.

Now, I want to thank you for listening to my side of this story. And, please use the attached **"FREE OFFICE VISIT"** prescription on your next visit (before the expiration date.) Also, please make sure you call ahead. Just call Stefi or me today at (262) 534-3767 to schedule your **FREE** office visit.

Thanks! *Marie*

P.S. I printed this letter on yellow paper because I'm telling you my story about our Yellow Pages ad. Pretty cool, eh? By the way, Monopoly Man came back after lunch. He's doing great now. Bye!!!

FIGURE 6.1: Nielsen Exhibit, continued

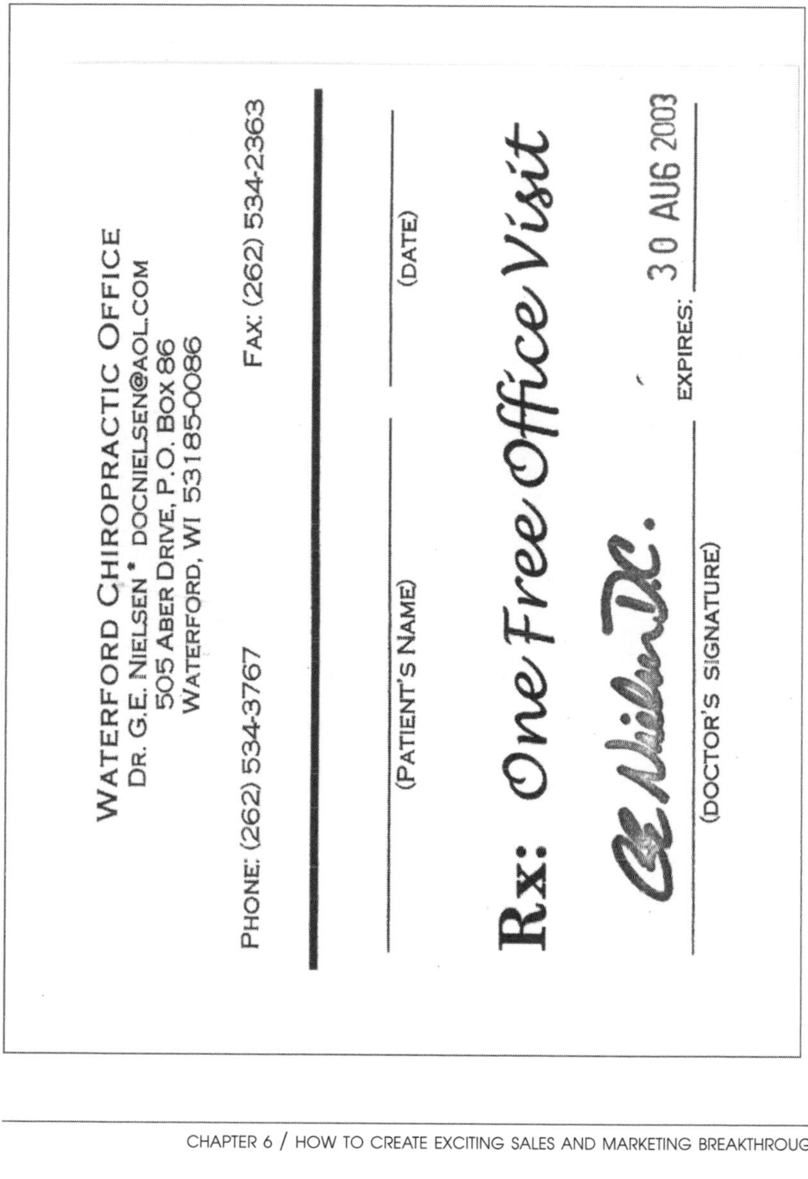

WATERFORD CHIROPRACTIC OFFICE
DR. G.E. NIELSEN * DOCNIELSEN@AOL.COM
505 ABER DRIVE, P.O. BOX 86
WATERFORD, WI 53185-0086

PHONE: (262) 534-3767   FAX: (262) 534-2363

_____
(PATIENT'S NAME)

_____
(DATE)

Rx: *One Free Office Visit*

_____   EXPIRES: 3 0 AUG 2003
(DOCTOR'S SIGNATURE)

FIGURE 6.1: Nielsen Exhibit, continued

ATTENTION: Auto & Work Accident Victims

Thinking About A Chiropractor?

(We Tried Dr. Nielsen's Office For You!)

BY STEFI MARIE & ERICA ALEXANDER
Freelance Health Correspondents

(WATERFORD, WI) -- You could call any chiropractor when you're in pain. However, we found a doctor we really like...and we want to tell you why you should call Dr. Nielsen today.

Why did we choose Dr. Nielsen? We were referred! If you ask around, there is a good chance that one of your friends (or neighbors) has been treated at Dr. Nielsen's Waterford office.

Four Reasons To See Dr. Nielsen Today

1) Dr. Nielsen treats your pain without using drugs, needles, or surgery.

2) Dr. Nielsen has treated hundreds of auto and work accident cases for over 19 years in Waterford. Using specialized training and equipment, he's uniquely qualified to treat your pain.

3) Dr. Nielsen's experienced staff will also manage the paperwork with your insurance company to make sure you get ALL the care you deserve to relieve your pain.

4) If you need an attorney referral, Dr. Nielsen knows many lawyers in this area and he can help you find one based upon your specific needs.

How To Get A FREE Copy Of Dr. Nielsen's New e-Book Of Simple & Easy Home Remedies

Dr. Nielsen has been in Waterford for over nineteen years, and he's well known for recommending "quick & easy" pain-relieving home remedies to his patients and friends. In fact, you can download Dr. Nielsen's FREE e-book of simple home remedies: *"Wisconsin Folk Medicine"* at www.docnielsen.com by clicking: "Free Stuff".

A Quick Home Remedy For Pain Relief

Use Ice Instead Of Heat. Applying heating pads may cause you to swell and become more inflamed. Apply an ice pack for 15 minutes instead of a heating pad. *When in doubt, use ice!*

What To Do When Your Favorite Home Remedies Don't Work

However, sometimes even your favorite home remedies don't work. Then it's time to call Dr. Nielsen's Waterford office at (262) 534-3767 or 1-800-359-3765 (24 Hrs.) to schedule your FREE *"Injury Severity Evaluation™"*.

Your time is valuable, and Dr. Nielsen's clinic is convenient for busy people who just don't have time to wait. It's located one block south of the old Sentry Food Store, right behind the 76 Gas Station...and he's open 6 days a week. We know you'll like Dr. Nielsen, his friendly staff, and his great service!

Here's What To Do Right Now

First, call Dr. Nielsen's office right now at (262) 534-3767 to make your first appointment. Then, print out your New Patient Forms. You can find them at *www.docnielsen.com*. Third, complete your New Patient Forms at home to save time. Fourth, bring your completed New Patient Forms with you on your first visit. And you can also...

Call Dr. Nielsen's "Injury Hotline" Today For More Info & A Free Recorded Message

It's easy to get more information about whiplash injuries, work accidents, hand and wrist problems. All you have to do is call Dr. Nielsen's office right now toll-free: 1-800-675-5831 (24 Hrs) for a free recorded message. Your FREE info packet will be sent by First Class Mail the same day you call. Oh, and don't forget to download your FREE e-book of simple home remedies at *www.docnielsen.com.*

Waterford Chiropractic Office
Dr. G.L. Nielsen * Email: docnielsen@aol.com
Internet Web Site: *www.docnielsen.com*
505 Aber Drive * P.O. Box 86
Waterford, WI * 53185-0086

Ph: (262) 534-3767

CHAPTER 7

Why and How to Sell
Your Way Through Life

You can succeed if others do not believe in you.
But you cannot succeed if you do not believe in yourself.

—Dr. Sidney Newton Bremer, Successful Achievement

I n this chapter, I'm not going to attempt to teach you how to sell—that deserves an entire book and then some—but I am going to make a case for your becoming a master salesperson.

You probably don't like the idea of being a salesperson. If you're like many people, you may think of salespeople as fast talkers—people who talk you into things. You may look at sales as combative: somebody has to lose for the salesman to win. And you perhaps believe that you can't learn to sell, that there really are such things as "born" salespeople. Finally, like many people, you might think that selling is unimportant in your chosen business.

I am here to tell you that these ideas are all false and must be corrected. If you expect to make any money as an entrepreneur, the mastery of selling is absolutely necessary.

Changing Your Attitudes about Selling

Myth #1: Selling Is Just Fast Talking

Selling has more to do with listening than talking. Tests done with telemarketers have demonstrated that those who listened twice as much as they talked wound up booking five times as many appointments. Selling is empathy in action.

Myth #2: Selling Sets Up a Win/Lose Situation

Selling can have winners and losers, but it doesn't have to be that way. Personally, my type of selling is win/win; the person buying my ideas, products, or services benefits at least as much as I do. The most successful salespeople uncover, clarify, and fulfill people's strongest needs and desires. My speaking colleague Zig Ziglar's most famous quotation is, "You can get anything in life you want by helping enough other people get what they want." Actually, you can get not only anything you want, you can get *everything* you want that way.

Myth #3: Sales Ability Is Hereditary

Selling is a combination of scientific and mechanical processes that can be learned by anybody, combined with the human qualities of compassion, empathy, and enthusiasm that exist—or at least potentially exist—in everybody.

The late Mark McCormack, super sports agent and author of *What They Don't Teach You at Harvard Business School*, looked at it from a different angle. He said that most people are born sales-people but that we "unlearn" it as we grow up. If you stop to think about it, most kids do have good sales instincts. They're not afraid to ask for what they want, persistently.

I suggest that you, too, are a born salesperson; that you already possess great sales instincts, even if you are suppressing them, and that you have the ability to release those instincts and to add new sales skills. With the combination of what you have inside naturally and what you can learn, you can become a master salesperson.

Myth #4: Selling Isn't Important to Every Business

Many books on business would have you believe that companies fail because of poorly selected locations, ill-prepared management, even bad bookkeeping. I think this is all B.S. *Businesses fail, more often than not, because the owners sit on their butts waiting for something to happen rather than going out and selling.* You can sell your way out of a lot of the trouble entrepreneurs typically stumble into if you have confidence and competence to sell.

But When Can I Stop Selling?

I used to look forward to the time that I might be able to take a break from selling. But that's the wrong attitude. As entrepreneurs, we have to be in the selling mode 100% of the time, so we might as well enjoy it.

Entrepreneurs actually need to do more selling than many salespeople. We have to sell and resell ourselves on our ideas, goals, plans, and decisions each and every day. We have to sell our associates and our employees on doing the things we want done, the way we want them done, when we want them done.

We have to sell our salespeople on our products, our services, our ideas, our leadership, themselves, their futures, on selling. We have to sell our vendors and suppliers that what we want done can be done, can be done by them, should be done by them, can be done when we need it done, and can be done at reasonable costs, under favorable terms. We have to sell our accountants and lawyers on our strategies. We have to sell to our bankers, our lenders, and investors.

> The decision is not whether to sell. The decision is whether to do it masterfully and whether to enjoy it.

I am not just talking about face-to-face selling either. Most advertising is better viewed as selling in print, most of what we call marketing better viewed as selling in media. Everything in business should be critically analyzed through the prism of *does it sell?*

Consider "environment," just as an example. I teach chiropractors and dentists to chuck the magazines out of the reception room, to replace them with testimonial and success story books, before-and-after photo albums, and health-related books, and to decorate the walls with framed patient testimonials instead of paintings. My contention is there are only three things that a patient should be doing while in the office: getting treated and getting well, getting educated, and getting motivated to refer. In other words, being sold.

Owners of service businesses, such as my coaching client Chet Rowland who owns the most successful independent pest control company in Florida, engineer huge leaps in profits when they convert ALL their employees—including the technicians in the field—to sales professionals.

The Two Most Important Sales You'll Ever Make

I believe the most important sale you'll ever make in your life is selling yourself on selling.

The day you commit to a life of selling can be the day that turns your life around. When you start viewing your activities in the context of making sales, you'll get much more done, much faster, and much more effectively.

The second most important sale is selling you on you. Do you really believe you have what it takes to succeed as an entrepreneur? How you feel about yourself and how you see yourself (self-image) combine to regulate what you permit yourself to do and be, much like the thermostat on the wall regulates temperature. No one can outperform his or her own self-esteem or self-image. (For more information about this important subject, visit www.psycho-cybernetics.com.)

How to Bridge the Confidence Chasm

For new entrepreneurs, and sometimes for experienced entrepreneurs, there can be a wide gap between the capabilities a person thinks he has and the capabilities he perceives necessary for the tasks ahead. Facing that chasm can be as intimidating as standing at the edge of the Grand Canyon and contemplating an Evel Knievel motorcycle leap.

It has consistently been my experience that people underestimate themselves and overestimate what's necessary for the success they seek. The millionaire entrepreneurs that I know are not much smarter or more knowledgeable than the average person on the street, nor are they gifted or somehow preordained for exceptional achievement. In many cases, they're not even as smart as most people. Believe me, I've met some pretty dumb rich people. Just about anybody *could* do what they do, it's just that few *will* do what they do.

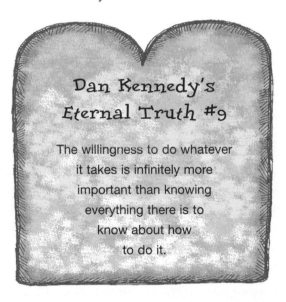

Dan Kennedy's Eternal Truth #9

The willingness to do whatever it takes is infinitely more important than knowing everything there is to know about how to do it.

One good way to bridge the confidence chasm is to make a point of discovering how little the so-called experts and superstars actually do know. You'll be shocked, as I was shortly after I'd determined that I would build a business as a speaker and seminar leader.

I had given a lot of speeches to sales organizations, clubs, and other groups around Phoenix, was making about $10,000.00 a month in a way I believed to be primitive and difficult, and had decided it was time to hang around the real pros at the National Speakers Association to find out how this business was really supposed to be run. By the end of the first afternoon workshop I attended, I was thoroughly depressed—not at how much I yet had to learn but at how little the "superstars" knew! I got over my disappointment when it dawned on me that I was a whole lot farther along than I'd guessed and that I was clearly "qualified" to be a big success in this field.

There were many speakers there who were infinitely better than I was on the platform. But I could find none better at selling.

This is not meant as any kind of criticism of this association. I've had similar experiences with other groups. I've discovered, over and over again, that the chasm between my self-assessment and my perception of the experience of the wizards is easily bridged.

More recent was my entry into the infomercial and video production business. When I went to my first couple of Hollywood videotapings, I was pretty intimidated and eager to see the highly paid geniuses at work. To make a long story short, I've discovered that the technical know-how was easily purchased and that the more important sales and marketing know-how could come from me just as easily as anyone else. Shortly after that, I produced my first infomercial from scratch, and I did everything: wrote the script, rented the facility, hired the crew, supervised the taping, and edited the show, all for about 15% of the typical Hollywood budget. That show made the client quite rich, generating millions of dollars and airing continuously for eight years.

This is not to say that I haven't made some mistakes in this business. I have, and I've made big ones. But I also see the most experienced, supposedly brightest experts in this field making big mistakes now and then, too. Now, based on my actual track record, I'm looked at as one of those top experts. In fact, over the years, I've been paid more than a million dollars for infomercial work alone. I still can't operate a videocamera. I can't even get the clock on my VCR to stop blinking.

The bottom line is that success really is simple. There are commonsense fundamentals that make up 80% of the essence of each and every business. These fundamentals are transferable from one field to another. Once you grasp these, it's not difficult to collect or hire the other 20% of specialized knowledge.

You can hire expertise and experience at surprisingly low cost. Some of the smartest people in the world are working for wages, employed by companies founded by "dumb" entrepreneurs. You can also learn what you need to know about the specialized

Dan Kennedy's Eternal Truth #10

The ability to win is easily transferred from one business to another.

aspects of any given business in a hurry. What you bring to the table, and what is not so easily duplicated or obtained, is entrepreneurial guts.

Earl Nightingale, one of the most famous success philosophers of all time and founder of the Nightingale-Conant Corporation, once pointed out that if there were no successful examples for you to observe, you could just as easily learn how to succeed from unsuccessful people! Note what they do, and then do the opposite. That idea applies to every business group I've ever been a part of or consulted in: about 5% of the people in the group rake in 95% of the money. The other 95% of the group represent sustained mediocrity. They have lousy work habits, poor self-images, and vague and disorganized goals; waste huge quantities of time; and lack imagination and initiative. By carefully listening to them, you can identify what not to think about and talk about; by observing their actions, you can see what not to do.

The confidence chasm gets a lot smaller as you realize how basic bridging the gap is.

Another Important Sale

You can't sell what you haven't bought.

I'll often ask business people these three questions:

1. If you were the customer, would buying from you be the clear, inarguably best choice?
2. Why should I do business with you instead of any of your competitors? In fact, why should I do business with you vs. any and every other option available to me? (That's my original, proprietary, copyright-protected Unique Selling Proposition Question. You ought to pull it out of this book,

write it boldly on a 4" x 6" card and tack it up some place you see a lot.)

3. Is your product or service a lot better than anything else out there? How?

It may surprise you to know that most people can't answer these questions. They hem and haw, stammer and stutter, and, at best, mutter some goofy slogan.

If you can't answer these questions, you're probably not completely sold on the superiority of what you're selling, and if you're not sold, you can't sell.

In his great book *How I Raised Myself From Failure To Success In Selling*, Frank Bettger revealed that enthusiasm made the difference for him. But I don't believe in *acting* enthusiastic; I believe in *being* enthusiastic. And that requires good reasons. You need to structure or restructure your business, product, service, idea, or promise so that *you* are sold on the superiority of what you offer. After that, convincing others is easy.

To be convincing, you have to be convinced.

Now I'll Make a Sale

Seems appropriate, in a chapter about selling, for me to sell something, doesn't it?

Now, if you'll gift me just a couple minutes of your time, I'll try and make a sale. I would like you to go back to your bookstore or go online to Amazon.com or B&N.com, or wherever you go to buy your books, and get yourself a copy of the companion book to this one, *No B.S. Sales Success*. It is as important for business owners who don't fully accept that they are salespeople as it is for acknowledged professional salespeople. In this book, I cut through all the complicated, theoretical B.S. about sales, persuasion, and influence, and give you a very simple, streamlined approach that works. You'll also get a short course in what I call "Takeaway Selling," which links to the discussion about "positioning" earlier in this book. I'll wager it's one of the best books on selling you will ever read and that you'll rate it worth far more than its cost, an important addition to your library. If you differ and if you wish, I'll personally buy your copy from you.

CHAPTER 8

Key People
for Your Company

Your friends may come and go, but your enemies accumulate.

—COACH BILL FOSTER

Very few people can or want to go it totally alone. Even the Lone Ranger had Tonto. Tarzan had Jane *and* a chimp. There are many reasons for this urge to surround yourself with others, some good, some not so good.

Some entrepreneurs build up excess staff, for example, out of feelings of insecurity, a feeling that theirs is more of a real business if there are a bunch of employees milling around. Many want associates and employees to counter the stark loneliness of entrepreneurship compared to the camaraderie of a corporate environment. Others need a cheering section. But these are all poor reasons for taking on partners, associates, or employees.

Recently, a client of mine returned home to meet with his accountant after an arduous, weeklong business travel adventure. After the meeting, he fired his 14 employees, put his 6,000-square-foot office complex up for lease, and went home to announce to his wife that he was moving his business back into the spare bedroom where it had started a decade before. One year later, he had done about 40% as much gross business as the previous year but kept more money for himself and his family. And he calculated that the extra hours of work he had to do for himself were offset three-to-one by time saved not dealing with his employees' personal problems, petty disputes with co-workers, and so on.

Another client bought out his two partners, who were the "Mr. Inside" guys while he was "Mr. Outside," drumming up business. He had a lot of fear about how he would manage things without them, but growing differences of opinion had become intolerable. To his shock, employees, vendors, even clients began telling him horror stories they'd been unwilling to talk about when the "ogres" were there. He replaced the two partners, who had each been getting fat salaries plus a percentage of profits, and each of their secretaries—four in all—with one new assistant, starting at only $35,000.00 a year.

Of course, not every business lends itself to such dramatic downsizing and simplified operation, but the point remains: too often, entrepreneurs take on people for the wrong reasons.

The best reason to add people to your venture is to contribute to increased *profits*. There was a time when I would have said that this was the only good reason, but there are others. You may choose, for example, to employ a person who makes your life easier, handles problems for you, and frees up some of your time for personal or family activities, even if, in hard dollars, that person represents expense, not profit. As long as you do that knowingly and deliberately, fine.

The other very good reason is to obtain creativity and experience you cannot provide. Most successful entrepreneurs develop and depend on a small circle of close, trusted associates from their network of partners, key employees, friends, family, even peers, for input, encouragement, and support.

Andrew Carnegie described the formation of such a team as "the mastermind concept." The greatest caution that Carnegie, and his protégé, Napoleon Hill, had to offer was about choosing carefully the people you include in your mastermind group or groups. The need for harmony, these men pointed out, is crucial.

In the entertainment world, a great team of masterminds made the *Tonight Show* an enormously successful television institution: Johnny Carson, Ed McMahon, and producer Fred

> In a way, belonging to my Inner Circle, especially at Gold Level or Gold Plus, is belonging to a long-distance mastermind group. I serve as a focal point or clearinghouse for the questions, problems, experiences, and discoveries of thousands of marketing-oriented entrepreneurs worldwide. My Gold/VIP and Platinum Inner Circle groups function as true mastermind groups, meeting for eight days each year.

DeCordova. In the infomercial business, I'm proud to have been part of the "brain trust" at Guthy-Renker Corporation that yielded dozens of successful infomercials such as *Personal Power with Tony Robbins*, the *Victoria Principal Skin Care Program*, Pro-Activ acne treatment, and the *Entrepreneur* magazine show, *Be Your Own Boss*. Different Guthy-Renker projects involve different members of a mastermind group of about two dozen people, including writers, producers, technical people, product development people, and marketing consultants. For my rare independent productions, I, too, have a pool I draw from for a quality mastermind group for each project.

You will no doubt be eager to develop a team of people you can work with in your business. But it's important to exercise caution in assembling your team, and you should be very aware of the problems that can arise. You may also want to organize a "mastermind group" outside your business that you can bounce ideas off of and look to for support.

Take Off Your Rose Colored Glasses

Because entrepreneurs tend to be optimists, they generally view people in their best light. But that may be unrealistic, and regrettably, this attitude can lead to frustration more often than to fulfillment. As hard as it may be to understand, some people just do not want to be motivated, to be helped, to be coached, to improve. And, when you try to force it on them, bad things usually happen.

On more than one occasion, I have made the mistake of bringing on a partner with unrealistic expectations. In one case, I brought in a close, personal friend as an executive of a company I had acquired, but I did so without considering the full picture. I saw him as I wanted him to be, not as he really was, and I tried to make him into someone he wasn't prepared to be. The result was the destruction of a friendship and significant expense to me.

Enduring, successful partnerships are as rare as pro athletes without rap sheets. DeVos and VanAndel at Amway come to mind, my clients Bill Guthy and Greg Renker, then my mind goes blank. Michael Eisner was unable to keep his close, partner-like relationship with Jeffrey Katzenberg at Disney, and heck, that's "the happiest place on earth"! Certainly, we can roam through recent business history and cite far more partnerships and top leadership teams that have come apart at the seams than we can those with longevity.

Having had my 22-year marriage suddenly and surprisingly end, which was a double-whammy of losing my wife and business partner, I have some cautionary advice about having a business partnership with your spouse. Although we were fortunate to be able to reach an amicable end to our relationship and even now have an ongoing business relationship, this may not always be possible. So, by all means, hope for the best, but prepare in advance for the worst.

Do not permit your spouse or anyone else to become indispensable to your business. There should only be one person who is indispensable. You.

If It's Not Meant to Be . . .

Very few business relationships go the distance. That's why the smartest entrepreneurs develop dissolution agreements at the start of relationships. I know that I will never again take on a partner without such an agreement.

When it becomes evident to you that you have a "cancer" in your business, you cannot afford to hesitate or procrastinate for even a day. Cut out the cancer before it spreads. And this goes double for cancer within your mastermind group. If your relationship with a key person deteriorates and there is no hope for recovery, you cannot afford the luxury of keeping that person around, even for one more minute.

When you "divorce," do it as decisively, cleanly, and courteously as possible. Avoiding unnecessary animosity is important for many reasons. It's an energy drain. It can block sensible negotiation and settlement. Biting your lip until it bleeds for a few days while getting the person out is infinitely preferable to bleeding for years from vengeful negative attacks. If there's anything reasonable you can do to diffuse the other person's anger, do it. On the other hand, if bloody battle is unavoidable, make it quick. Do what you must do to protect your business. That *is* your responsibility.

How to Choose Your Key People

Many new entrepreneurs don't really *choose* key associates; they anoint a spouse, unemployed brother-in-law, or buddy at work for no reason other than the fact that they are spouse, brother-in-law, or buddy. This is no way to hire your vice president.

In any case, every entrepreneur needs one support person. I work with a lot of clients who are essentially one person operations, generating from $1 million or $2 million to as much as $20 million a year. In the information marketing/mail-order field, where I have lots of clients, this is very doable. However, every one of these still needs and has at least one back-up person. The really smart ones have two, for reasons I'll discuss later.

Entrepreneurs tend to leap between extremes of refusing to delegate vs. delegating tasks wildly, sloppily, and hastily. The most important person in the entrepreneur's business life will be very good at running behind, scooping up the pieces, and making sure initiatives get implemented. This key person has to cheerfully accept all this responsibility and, often, read the entrepreneur's mind.

That calls for four strong characteristics:

1. Ability to accept responsibility
2. Relatively low need for reassurance and recognition
3. Ability to cooperate
4. Ability to confront problems with maturity

This person can't worry about who gets the credit for success or who gets blamed for mistakes. He has to be secure enough about his own worth to not need recognition from afar. He needs to be very results oriented.

This person also needs to be good at creating and fostering cooperation among others. Because the entrepreneur often moves very quickly and assertively, he sometimes runs over other people's sensibilities. Somebody has to clean up that mess, too. (OK, take out the word "sometimes" and substitute "almost always.")

Behind just about every high-profile, highly successful entrepreneur, you'll find several of these key support people. These behind-the-scenes people are much like assistant coaches of major basketball or football teams. The high-profile head coach does the interviews, has the camera's eye, and gets the glory (or the criticism). But the head coach couldn't get through a game without the team of assistant coaches.

Last, the entrepreneur's key associate has to have great maturity in his handling of problems. This means no panic, no emotional overreactions, just the calm voice of reason. I know several entrepreneurs who have just such people working with them, and they are very fortunate. One real estate broker I know pays his executive secretary $125,000.00 a year plus perks. Some of the few people who know of this think it's outrageous, but it is good value for what she does—and good business.

The Worst Number in Any Business—and What to Do about It

Here is an advanced piece of information that, until now, I've talked about only at my high-priced seminars for entrepreneurs: the worst number in business is *one*.

One is a very bad number, anywhere you find it.

If *one* client accounts for a disproportionate percentage of your revenue or profits, that's dangerous. If *one* media produces a disproportionate percentage of your customers, you are subject to being summarily put out of business. If *one* product accounts for a disproportionate percentage of sales, you are horribly vulnerable to competition.

Clients leave even when they shouldn't. When I ran a custom manufacturing business, a large client left us even though there were no quality or service problems. We had many times bent over backwards to meet his emergency needs, even carried him for months at a time when he couldn't pay. He switched vendors to save one half of one cent per unit. He said, "Biz is biz."

Another large client left us, bluntly, because the sales rep of the competing company was having sex with him.

Media gets taken away. TV infomercials were once legal, then outlawed, then legalized again. Recently, businesses have been thrown into trauma by new laws severely restricting use of fax for marketing purposes, e-mail for marketing purposes, and the Do Not Call list for telemarketing.

Products get knocked off, patents expire, copyrights get violated. It is very hard these days to sustain product exclusivity.

But by far, the worst *one* in a business is one key employee. If you are crossing a massive, barren desert and have only one horse, even if he kicks you, bites you, bucks you off, and craps on you, you can't shoot him. But if you have two . . . .

My advice—which sadly, I haven't always followed—to my clients is: never have only one person fulfilling any critical, key role. Have none or two, but never one. That way if you must shoot one, you can.

A number of clients have ignored this advice and told me how much they wish they hadn't, how much cheaper it would have been to pay the two salaries than to cope with the mess of the one's sudden departure. One of my coaching members, an investment manager, is in this category. He let one key, trusted person have all the contact with clients, then when that employee had to be axed, he had to step in and deal with chaos and even lost some clients. Now every client has equal contact with two key people.

Many other clients have followed the advice and thanked me profusely.

CHAPTER 9

Working with Lawyers
and Accountants

The first thing we do, let's kill all the lawyers.

—WILLIAM SHAKESPEARE, *HENRY VI*

I have spoken at the Lawyers Marketing Group's annual conference, and that company purchased my *Ultimate Sales Letter* and
Ultimate Marketing Plan books to give to all the attorneys in
attendance. In my coaching groups, I have four attorneys, three
from the United States, one from Canada, and one who is a marketing consultant to other attorneys. As a speaker, I have appeared on
programs with famous lawyers Alan Dershowitz and Gerry Spence.
I confess to admiring Spence's masterful persuasive abilities, and I
recommend his book *How To Win An Argument Every Time*.

Here and now, I apologize to all entrepreneurs for helping
attorneys. I'm sorry. My defense? I take special joy in taking *their*
money.

The relationships between entrepreneurs and their lawyers, accountants, and bankers tend to be rocky at best. Most entrepreneurs I know harbor intense dislike for these people, including the ones they pay, and all their colleagues. Believe me, I understand this dislike. On the other hand, I have faced the reality that you cannot survive in today's business environment without relationships with these people. It's OK not to like them, but it's still important to be able to elicit productive results from them.

How to Be Litigious without Buying Your Lawyer a Yacht

I have been accused of being litigious, which means I often threaten to sue and file lawsuits. I have, on a number of occasions, been quick to threaten and quick to proceed; it's often proved to be the best way to avoid being pushed around. I've discovered that most people as well as many companies have no real stomach for legal warfare. They know how costly and time-consuming it can be.

I have been more restrained in this area recently than in earlier years. Some of that is the prevailing of a cooler head, a lot of it the opportunity to be much more selective in who I permit myself to be involved with. However, still, there are times when nothing short of a lawsuit will do.

Al Capone is credited with saying, "You can get a lot with a kind word and a smile, but you can get a lot more with a kind word, a smile, and a gun." Some people understand only power and force.

What to Do if You Are in a Fight

One of the most time-consuming legal weapons is called *discovery*. This allows you to subpoena opponents' records, interrogate them under oath, and serve them with written interrogatories that must be completed within a certain period of time. An inter-rogatory is a written set of questions, pages long, prying into every imaginable aspect of the opponent's business and personal life. If there is a possibility of your being awarded damages from your lawsuit, you have the right to discover, in advance, the nature and location of all the opponent's assets. You can ask for detailed information about income, bank accounts, and personal and family assets. Like an inventory of the wife's jewelry, the amounts in the kids' piggy-banks.

With this approach, you can consume immense amounts of the opponent's time and force public disclosure of information he would rather not make public. Also, dropping a 200-page interrogatory on an opponent's spouse can make for a very inter-esting evening in their home. Used properly, the interrogatory is often the only shot you have to fire.

Some lawyers are reluctant to drop this big a bomb. I advise against employing timid or polite lawyers. If the time comes when you must sue somebody, it's important to find a lawyer who will go for the jugular.

In a number of conflicts, people have instantly become more reasonable and respectful as soon as they've realized that I was prepared to bring in the legal beagles and start discovery. I signify this by sending copies to my lawyer of the correspondence I have with the other party, and sometimes, copying that party my memo to my lawyer. Using only this method, I've settled in my favor a lot of problems.

Just for example, I used this method to settle a dispute with a trade magazine that had made a mistake with the photos in an advertisement we placed. When the magazine billed us $1,800.00, I wrote to the publisher expressing my dissatisfaction. When that got nowhere, I sent a second letter indicating my refusal to pay any amount and describing how the deficient ad had probably damaged us at a trade show. That second letter indicated a copy had gone to my lawyer. Soon afterward, I got an offer from the publisher to settle for $900.00. I counter-offered, again noting that a copy went to my lawyer, and settled for $500.00.

Why, you ask, did I do all the work myself? Why not just turn it over to the lawyer from the beginning?

First of all, although some of my companies have had lawyers on retainer, I do not have a blanket retainer arrangement. Carbon-copying costs me nothing. Having a lawyer handle it costs me $200.00 an hour. Second, I wanted to rattle my sabers, not actually wind up in battle. Keep in mind that your interests and your lawyer's interests rarely coincide. In the matter of the $1,800.00 bill described above, I would have had to nudge, push, and check up on the lawyer a half-dozen times to get it handled. Lawyers tend to deal each day with only those matters that have escalated to crisis, so a case like mine would have been put on the back burner forever. It would have cost me more than the $1,300.00 that I saved to get it done.

Using a similar threat of litigation, I have, at various times, stopped a competitive company's salesperson from spreading rumors, got an insurance company to pay off nearly $250,000.00 in claims on a technically lapsed policy, got an undesirable equipment lease terminated without penalty, reduced and compromised bills, and collected past-due balances.

My objective through all this has been to win cheaply and quickly. And in 25-odd years of using this approach, I've wound up in actual lawsuits only four times: settling twice and litigating twice.

Your Turn Can Come

It comes as a seismic shock to many entrepreneurs how easily and frequently they can be threatened with lawsuits. Anybody can sue you at anytime for anything. Sure, you have recourse in most cases where the suit filed against you proves baseless and you can demonstrate cash damages as a result. By that time, though, you've had your business and family disrupted, tied up money in legal fees and costs, and consumed a fortune in antacids.

When you get attacked, most lawyers will want to react slowly, cautiously, and by the book. I've found, however, that when threatened or served with a lawsuit, the best defense is a very fast, very strong, even a little wild-eyed-and-foaming-at-the-mouth, kick-butt offense. Push your lawyer to run straight at them.

Dan Kennedy's
Eternal Truth #11

Talk is cheap...
until you hire a lawyer.

Legal problems are a part of business. The old idea that nobody has legal problems unless they deserve them is as out-of-date as handshake agreements and leaving the back door unlocked while you take an evening stroll down to the ice cream parlor.

When You Must Really Use a Lawyer

Keep this in mind: don't lose control. Don't be intimidated. Don't let yourself leave with a pat on the head, a reassuring word, and unanswered questions. You must understand everything about your situation. Take nothing for granted. Insist on being an informed participant in the strategy process. If the lawyer wants to tell you what to do rather than educate you about your options and their ramifications and help you make your decision, run.

You must manage your lawyer just as you would any other employee. Be very clear about fees, costs, and how the relationship is to work. Follow up on every phone conversation or meeting with a written letter, "just to confirm what we agreed to do," and use this memo to reference and enforce deadlines. Be polite and considerate, of course, but firm. You are the boss—act like it.

Some lawyers will work effectively with you in this kind of relationship. Some will not. There are plenty to choose from.

Putting a Wall around Your Castle and Alligators in the Moat

If you have or appear to have assets, are or appear to be successful, you are a target.

The business owner is in constant peril of lawsuits from employees, associates, investors, customers, vendors, and passersby.

Most entrepreneurs are negligent, chronic procrastinators about asset protection. It is akin to home security systems: well over half are purchased and installed only after the home is burglarized. However, we are talking about more than the loss of your TV and having your "undies" pawed over.

There are more than 90 million lawsuits filed in the United States in an average year. We have more attorneys per capita than any other nation: 700,000 attorneys and 130,000 more in law schools as I write this. They all need work. They all need somebody to sue. Like you.

One of my clients, attorney William Reed, has written a very good primer on the subject of asset protection, *Bullet-Proof Asset Protection,* and I recommend you read it. You should also consult with an astute commercial property/casualty insurance agent. You should address asset safeguarding before you even feel you need it. After you need it, it's too late.

Strange Creatures, Accountants

Accountants can be almost as maddening as lawyers to the entrepreneur, but for different reasons. The temperament and thinking of someone happy to sit in an office crunching numbers is diametrically opposed to the personality of the go-get-'em entrepreneur.

Still, you need a good accountant.

What makes a good accountant? The entrepreneurial joke is "You ask, 'What's this number?' And the good accountant says, 'What would you like it to be?'" That's amusing right up until the first tax audit. My own working definition, which may or may not be exactly right for you, is that a good accountant imposes a reasonable degree of discipline on your record-keeping and is very knowledgeable, informative, and helpful in the area of tax law— where your biggest risks and biggest costs can occur.

I have had good ones and bad ones, cheap ones and expensive ones, and my advice is find and hire good, even if expensive.

The one mistake never to make is to put the bean counters in charge of harvesting beans. A lot of companies are grown to a certain point by an entrepreneur, then turned over to accountant-types to manage. More often than not, they destroy it. It's quite common for an entrepreneur to sell a good company to a big, dumb company run by bean counters, then get to buy it back for a fraction of what he was paid for it in the first place!

Just as we entrepreneurs aren't very good at counting or keeping beans and a whole lot better at harvesting them, the accountants good at counting 'em are inept at harvesting.

Rearview Mirrors, Magnifying Glasses, and Binoculars

It's very important to understand that the kinds of numbers accountants and CPAs assemble and provide to you are "rearview mirror" numbers. They are historical. They tell you what has already happened in your business.

These numbers are useful in identifying what has gone awry, what needs to be fixed—such as a type of expense that has grown in terms of percentage of sales—what needs to be roped in, or what product or service is insufficiently profitable vs. others. That sort of thing. But with these numbers you are always fixing what has already occurred.

These numbers are also constructed more to satisfy tax authority requirements and meet general accounting norms than they are to help you manage your business more profitably.

You need "magnifying glass" numbers to make good, day-to-day, current decisions. That means what is happening, magnified, so you can clearly see and understand it. These numbers are foreign to most accountants. For example, two of the most important numbers in marketing are CPL, Cost Per Lead, and CPS, Cost Per Sale, and they need to be tracked by source. Most business owners cannot tell you what it costs them to acquire a new customer or to sell a particular product. Another vital number is

Incidentally, the entrepreneurs I've worked with over the years who make the most money and build the biggest fortunes are the ones who are very, very good at these magnifying glass numbers. So good, I can't stump them with a question. My former client, now retired, Len Shykind at U.S. Gold could, in moments, pull up any number you could ask for, with regard to the CPL or CPS from any of hundreds of different TV stations and dozens of magazines he advertised with, comparing day to day, month to month, time slot to time slot. A much bigger user of TV, Guthy-Renker, is comparably on top of these numbers. My coaching member Dr. Ben Altadonna, who markets seminars and information products to chiropractors, and my Platinum Member, client, and publisher of my newsletter, Bill Glazer, are both, to be impolite, down-right anal retentive about these numbers. They win big because they are.

TCV, Total Customer Value. You decide whether your business has short or long customer life, one year or ten years. But you have to know what a customer is worth in order to determine how much you are willing to pay to get one. These are the kinds of numbers that those of us in direct marketing understand, that most other types of entrepreneurs don't.

This is difficult for most entrepreneurs, because we hate crunching numbers. I love working with clients who do it well even though, personally, I'm mediocre at it, better than most by small margin. The worst entrepreneur I've ever seen at it, bar none, was an early mentor of mine, who constantly insisted, "If there's enough gross, there must be net around here somewhere." He was wrong. And broke a lot, even with gigantic grosses.

You also need "binocular numbers." These are predictions and forecasts into the future that may affect current decisions. These, of course, are the hardest to come by.

One way I use binoculars and approach this for each year is figuring up, listing, and forecasting all the income I can be reasonably sure of earning. The difference between that total and my goal must then be bridged. I can then start slicing that sum up and assigning pieces of it to different sources of income, different promotions I'll need to do. This is how I plan my year's schedule of activities.

Who Can You Count On?

In these necessary relationships, with accountants, lawyers, and other advisors, strive to make things the best they can be, but do everything you can to ensure against them turning to the worst they can be. And never lose sight of the fact that the only person you can completely rely on to protect your interests is you.

I teach that there are two things you NEVER delegate in a business. One is the marketing—the acquiring, optimizing, retaining, and multiplying of customers. That you want to be up to your armpits in, all the time.

The other is the checkbook and the important numbers affecting the checkbook.

I have four private clients who each, at different times, ignored my pleadings and turned their checkbooks over to someone else: a comptroller, an accountant. All four got screwed in slightly different ways.

I handle millions of dollars a year. I sign every check. By hand. And I pay attention to what I'm signing. I wouldn't do it any other way.

Another thing you want to pay attention to is your "white mail." To give credit where credit is due, I got this piece of advice from Gary Halbert, and it has served me well. I not only open and read my own mail, I occasionally swoop in, grab all the incoming mail, and go through every piece—especially correspondence from customers. If you don't, problems may be swept under the rug or mishandled, and eventually wind up biting you in the butt.

The bottom line is: you're on the hot seat all by yourself. It may look like you're surrounded by others, but don't be standing in their way en route to the lifeboats in a storm.

CHAPTER 10

Why Entrepreneurs Aren't
Managers—and What You
Can Do about It

*Never try to teach a pig to sing. You'll only annoy
the pig and get yourself covered with mud.*

—Unknown

L et me preface this chapter with a personal confession. My
ability to pick and hire good employees is roughly equivalent to my interest in having them. Zero. I am a far better
golfer, and I can't play golf. At one point, I had 43 employees. I
concluded I'd rather have daily root canal. Consequently, I have
structured my own businesses to function without them. In
recent years, I've had only one. In a distant office, not underfoot.

Many businesses would be better reconfigured to have fewer
people. But many still require them.

I have some observations and opinions, based in part on my
own pain and suffering and in part on what I've learned from

clients who are far, far more successful at managing employees than I am.

I feel fortunate that for most of my life I have operated businesses with a minimum number of employees. Today, I have one. But I have had 5, 10, 43. I've had father, mother, and brothers as employees. I've had my share of managerial experience.

At one point, I suddenly took over a company with 43 employees. The only management had been dictatorial and ineffective. There were massive quality control, productivity, and other problems. It was a hostile environment. I determined to do something about it all.

At the time, I had been doing a massive amount of reading about different management styles: Japanese management, open-door management, management by objectives, management by values, team-building, and building ownership mentality. Exciting buzzwords, all of them. Once again, however, I discovered that most of the folks writing these theories never managed anybody. Or they managed only in their memories, from a time when people latched onto a good job and then did everything in their power to keep it; when getting sacked was a red badge of humiliation. Times are different now.

So, I waded in with all this terrific theory and got my head handed back to me, with bloody claw marks all over it. I sewed it back on, stuck it in there again, and pulled out a bloody stump.

What have I learned from that experience and from working with clients beset with management problems? The big secret. And here it is: all the theories work wonderfully with wonderful people. But trying to teach pigs to sing or chickens to soar is tough, tough work.

For example, I've done a lot of consulting work with chiropractors. Typically, they have staffs of three to ten people who are all very important. Their contact with patients affects repeat business and referrals. Their attitudes affect the doctor's attitude, and these practices are attitude-driven businesses. I know doctors who bring their entire staffs to seminars, and there they are, smiling, happy, enthusiastic people, eager to do their jobs better. These doctors have incentive and bonus programs for their staffs. They set and work on team goals. They really have a team effort going. I also know doctors who have to pay and coerce their staffs to grudgingly go to a seminar. And there they are, stiff, frowning, restless, ants-in-their-pants, in and out of the room. These doctors try incentive and bonus programs, and they fail miserably. If these doctors try to talk "teamwork," the staff members mutter, "He's been to another seminar. It'll all blow over in a few days."

Using exactly the same management ideas, philosophies, methods, and strategies, one doctor will get incredibly good results; the other will be cut off at the knees.

Which brings us to several really tough, no B.S. management principles.

You Can't Teach a Pig to Sing

I repeat it again. You can apply the very same sound, proven motivational tools to ten people and get ten startlingly different results. Perhaps, theoretically, everybody and anybody can change and be inspired to change, but many "hard cases" just aren't worth the investment, as a practical matter.

Hire Slow, Fire Fast

This motto hangs on the wall of the CEO of one of the four largest national chains of weight-loss centers. But this philosophy is, of course, the exact opposite of what entrepreneurs tend to do. We hate to fire anybody. We're optimists, so we believe that everybody can be saved. We keep trying; we keep giving them one more chance. By the time we finally fire them, they walk away wondering why it took us so long, as do the other staff members.

Then, we have this vacuum to fill. We need that work done. So we grab the first warm body who passes by. And as they say, you have to kiss a lot of frogs to find a prince. I've gone through more than 55 people to get four good ones. Am I inept? Well, most entrepreneurs I know who have a good team get there by hiring, firing, hiring, firing, catching and throwing them back, and only very occasionally finding a "keeper."

Forget the Idea of Ownership Mentality

Listen, the only people who have ownership mentality are owners. That's that. Why should it be any other way? The main reason that managing people drives entrepreneurs crazy is all our silly, stubborn hopes, beliefs, and assumptions that "they" are like "us." They're not. If they were, they wouldn't be working for us—they'd be competing with us.

Some years back, when I had five employees, I achieved a new peace of mind by recalibrating my expectations for the performance of different people in different positions. Each position has different responsibilities and different definitions of satisfactory performance and of excellent performance, and in most cases, these positions do not require another *you* to meet these definitions.

I had two employees, for example, who just weren't "morning people." For years, it drove me bananas that they could not get to work on time. It drove a business partner of mine right over the edge. It became his mission to end their tardiness; he tried everything and failed. Otherwise, however, these two were exemplary employees. They perfectly fulfilled the performance requirements of their positions.

We arrived at the big breakthrough. We made a new deal. We told these two they could come and go and work pretty much whenever they wanted to work as long as all of the work that needed to get done got done on time. If they meandered in at 9:45 A.M., nobody thought anything of it. I didn't even ask or pay any attention to when they were there and when they were not. I

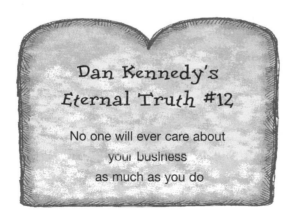

Dan Kennedy's
Eternal Truth #12

No one will ever care about
your business
as much as you do

wiped an entire chunk of anxiety and aggravation right off my plate. And it worked out magnificently.

But, make no mistake about it, they only excelled at meeting reasonable expectations for their positions.

How Your Employees Sabotage Your Marketing

I walked into the Subway restaurant near my house, about 1:30 P.M. on a weekday, to get a small sandwich and salad to go. There were two customers in a booth eating, no one in front of me at the counter. No "sandwich artist" visible. She emerged from the back room after several minutes, gave me a frustrated look, and greeted me:

"I can't get any work done today."

Gee, I was mistaken. I thought taking care of customers, making sandwiches, and stuffing cash into the register was her work. Bet the owner does, too. But he and I are both mistaken. Make this note: what we think her work is and what she thinks it is, what we think are her job priorities and what she thinks they are, two different things.

As she was nearly finished putting my order together, two new customers filed in, one right behind the other. The look on her face was pure disgust. In a voice loud enough for us all to hear, she said:

"It's been like this all day, one darned customer after another. How will I ever get to do my work?"

If you think this sort of thing only goes on in other peoples' businesses, you're dumber than a box of rocks. It goes on in yours, too, pretty much whenever your back's turned.

If you'd like a lengthy FREE REPORT, reprinted from my *No B.S. Marketing Letter*, about the 12 ways employees sabotage your marketing—and what you can do about it—go to www.nobsbooks.com/free. For now, know that whatever you aren't watching over like a hawk, you aren't getting.

You Can Only Expect What You Inspect

This is an old management axiom, and you've probably heard it before. Well, truth is truth, and if you want to stay sane, this is the way to manage.

Business owners don't want to believe their employees steal from them. Some don't even track their losses; they just stick their heads in the sand. And they're all wrong because most employees steal at some time. "Theft" takes many forms. It can be cash or merchandise, but it can also be the sabotage I just mentioned above, or time theft, or covering up for inept vendors. In direct, outright theft of cash and merchandise, most businesses lose 50% to 100% as much as the owners' ultimate net, pretax profits. In indirect theft, much more. This is a massive problem and a giant opportunity most business owners deny affects them.

About 2% of the population are incapable of ever stealing; they would rather starve. Another 2% will steal for a nickel; they are incapable of being honest. The remaining 96% of people will steal if the following three factors are present:

1. Need
2. Ability to rationalize their actions

3. Opportunity to get away with it

You cannot control the first two factors. Ask your employees if they need more money or if they need to take shortcuts in their work (another form of stealing), and most will answer yes. And most of us are pretty good at rationalizing our behavior. It often is expressed with words like, "He just bought a new hot car and lives high on the hog. We do all the dirty work around here— he'll never miss a few dollars."

However, you can control opportunity, and that is why you can only expect what you inspect.

I took over a custom products manufacturing company once with a serious quality-control problem. Over 30% of all jobs had something wrong with them. In one month, that dropped to 5%. How did I do it? I simply took the time to walk around the plant at different times, almost every day, randomly pulling samples out of production and checking them. As soon as everybody knew that the risk of detection was high, the error rate dropped.

This isn't rocket science; it's simple. It's applicable to any business.

Identify, Keep, Reward, and Motivate

Mike Vance, one of the top executives of the Disney Corporation for a number of years and now a management consultant, says that management is all about "developing people through work, while having fun."

I agree with him—I'm not a cynic after all! I believe that smart entrepreneur-managers provide environments, opportunities, and encouragement for growth to whatever degree is possible. I believe sensitivity toward the nonmonetary rewards of work is important. And I believe in having fun and offering bonuses, incentives, team goals, compete-against-yourselves contests, and, of course, an overall positive attitude.

In all businesses, unhappy people do poor work. It is part of good management to create the right environment in the workplace. There are people out there who would kill for an opportunity to work in a good job, for somebody who respects and appreciates them, who lets them grow with authority and responsibility, and who includes them in a team effort.

Quality people respond to quality management techniques, so you'll be involved in going through people, weeding out the uncooperative, identifying the gems—keeping, developing, involving, and rewarding the keepers. Because everything is always changing—people, their circumstances, your business, and you—this process will continue as long as you remain at the helm. Don't resent it, and do it as effectively as you can.

Recent Discoveries about All Employees

As you might imagine, "employee problems" is a hot topic whenever entrepreneurs gather. My own mastermind/coaching groups talk about it a lot, and out of these conversations came a couple discoveries that I now believe are key hiring criteria.

In comparing notes, we realized that we have each had one to several employees over a span of years who were terrific. More importantly, in comparing notes, we discovered a "secret" commonality shared by every one of those rare, terrific employees. So, finally, here is some good news—a "trick" you can use to greatly increase the likelihood of hiring a productive person.

The hidden factor we unearthed is that all our best employees grew up in a family business environment. Their parents owned some kind of a small business, and they saw how hard their parents worked. They worked in the business, too: they had exposure to dealing with customers and vendors and crises. The best of the best employees came from families that owned small restaurants.

I am sufficiently convinced of the validity of this factor that, if I were hiring people today, it'd be an absolute litmus test.

Another, similar "secret": the best employees to put in positions where they must handle incoming calls from new prospective customers or clients or otherwise interact directly with customers either have personal experience or have been around somebody with successful *direct* sales experience. That means they themselves or their father, mother, spouse, brother, or sister has sold something nose to nose, toes to toes, in homes or in showrooms, like vacuum cleaners, water filters, fire alarms, encyclopedias, or pool filters. This experience will have gotten them over the all-too-common "squeamishness" about selling. Employees who have that squeamishness will consciously or unconsciously sabotage or at least "short" what needs to be done to achieve optimum sales in your business.

Good People Can Make a Huge Difference

One of my coaching members, Lester Nathan, is the reigning expert advisor to America's independent pharmacy owners on successfully competing with the giant chains. Lester routinely helps pharmacy owners increase profits by 200% to 500% within the first 12 months he consults with them. He accomplishes this with three "tracks," one of which is improving the quality, capabilities, and motivation of the employees.

My Platinum Member Jay Geier routinely increases chiropractic and dental practices by comparable numbers solely by focusing on training, offering incentives, motivating, and policing the employees who take incoming calls from new patients.

The common ingredient in their approaches is superior training. Truth is, most employees are tossed into jobs with little or no real training, no scripts, and then are not held accountable for doing things as they ought to be done. Incredibly, in many businesses, even salespeople are going without sales training!

If you are going to have people, then you need to commit to doing everything you can to get, grow, and keep good ones.

What Works for You Is What's Right

Throw out the textbooks.

Five of the most successful CEOs I know have five dramatically different management styles. Their relationships with their people are different. Their beliefs about leadership are different. Their companies' environments feel different when you walk in. There *is* more than one right way.

Harold Geneen, who led the giant ITT, once said, "I have never come across a chief executive who tried, much less succeeded, running his company according to any set formula, chart, or business theory."

This is my most important message in this chapter on management: my way, that works for me, may very well fail miserably for you. You have to find your own way.

CHAPTER 11

How to Manage
Your Cash Flow

*The bankers asked for a statement.
I said I was "optimistic."*

—MARK VICTOR HANSEN, CO-AUTHOR, *CHICKEN SOUP FOR THE SOUL*

I t's amazing what you can do with cash. There have been times in my entrepreneurial experience when as little as a few thousand dollars of cash would have made a million-dollar difference. I once saved a million-dollar business from extinction with $25,000.00. There have also been times when a million dollars wouldn't have helped. But more often than not, it is better to have cash than not!

Happiness is positive cash flow. Many businesses struggle through years of losses before achieving profitability but survive thanks to positive cash flow. In business, cash flow buys the extra time necessary to win. Cash flow provides the staying power needed to invent, experiment, sort it all out, and, finally, wind up

Dan Kennedy's Eternal Truth #13

Cash is king.

with a winning system. It's not all that unusual for one new product, one new ad, or one sales breakthrough to swing a company from losing to winning. To outsiders, it may look like a lucky miracle. Actually, it's the logical result of a progression of experiments, failures, corrections, decisions, investments, and action.

Over the years, I've developed methods for increasing cash flow regardless of other aspects of a business. I call these my MCF Methods, Multiplied Cash Flow Methods.

The Five Keys to Multiplied Cash Flow

Reduce and Control Expenses

Most businesses have an incredible capacity to accumulate fat when the owners aren't looking. Phone bills, freight costs, office-supply expenses, shrinkage—all sorts of expenses can creep up.

To stay on top of it all, you should know what each category of expense should be in relation to your gross sales. You can determine these ratios by finding out what the norms are for your business or industry from your trade associations, reading reference materials, and relying on your own business experience. For example, let's say that in your business, long-distance phone costs should be between 5% and 7% of gross sales. If this month it comes out at 11%, you have reason to be alarmed.

Doesn't take much negligence to allow cost-creep. Vendors who get comfortable, who know they aren't being price shopped or questioned, inch up prices hoping you won't notice. An overworked employee starts sending nonurgent materials FedEx right along with the urgent outbounds. It was Everett Dirkson, the late senator from Illinois, who said about Congress, "A billion here, a billion there, pretty soon you've spent real money."

It's not my nature to pinch pennies, but I've learned that controlling expenses is another way of making money, no less important than any other. In your business, if it takes an average of $4.00 of sales to put $1.00 on the bottom line, it takes $4,000.00 to yield $1,000.00. That means $1,000.00 saved is the same as $4,000.00 sold.

Entrepreneurs tend to focus 100% of their energy on growing, not controlling, the business. Often they'll buy extra growth at higher and higher costs, making the incremental increase of questionable real value. Costs must be monitored and controlled and margins protected, or sales growth turns out to be a bad bargain at best, a danger to the business' survival at worst. You actually *can* grow your way to bankruptcy.

Get Financing Leverage

Obviously, the longer you can delay payment, the longer you have the use of that money. Big companies routinely take 60 or 90 days to pay their bills and get away with it because of their size. They use that "float" to make money. The small entrepreneur needs to keep this in mind and delay payments whenever possible without damaging credit ratings. Here are a few tips for accomplishing this feat.

- *Never pay bills early.* If you ever do have a cash crunch, this pattern will be to your detriment because your creditors will be spoiled and judge you more harshly. Pay on time but never early. Paying early is a dangerous precedent to set.
- *Negotiate extended terms in advance with suppliers.* Many entrepreneurs are pleasantly surprised at how easily this can be done. Vendors competing for your business will use financing to get it. Instead of terms of "net 30 days," you may be able to negotiate paying in two or three installments, like a third in 30 days, a third in 60 days, and a third in 90 days.
- *Conserve cash by leasing with deferred balloon payments.*
- *Refinance when you don't have to,* to consolidate debt and reduce monthly debt service.
- *If you have financed your business start-up with personal collateral and guarantees and a patchwork quilt of financing sources, strive to replace that with conventional business loans and lines of credit,* secured by the business, as soon as you can. With two years of profitability, growth, and a good payment track record, you can start working on this aggressively, shopping among banks if necessary.

Get Paid

Many businesses suffer from some or all of the following credit-management deficiencies:

- Loose credit policies

- No credit checks before granting credit
- No enforcement of credit limits
- Late invoicing
- Credit given to those with past-due balances
- No standardized collection procedures
- Unwillingness to get tough

If you are going to grant credit, you need to have a plan to prevent problems and resolve them when they do occur. Making sales doesn't matter much if you don't get paid. Take the following steps to implement your plan:

- Develop strict credit policies.
- Make each customer complete a credit application.
- Check the references.
- Consider joining a credit bureau and checking credit files.
- Set credit limits for each customer.
- Send your invoices out promptly.
- Implement a collection procedure beginning with the first of three warning notices out the 32nd day.
- Cut off past-due clients and only negotiate a "deal" as you see fit; do not keep granting credit to people who cannot or will not pay.
- Get tough when you have to; preserving the goodwill of a customer who can't or won't pay is silly.

This is all common sense, isn't it? So why do so many entrepreneurs do such lousy jobs of collecting the money owed them? Because while they are wearing one hat, trying to negotiate with vendors to get better terms, they develop great empathy for their customers. They find it difficult to switch attitudes when they switch hats.

A warning: invariably a business owner will play bank and carry a slow-pay account only to later have that client summarily leave and switch to a competitor without a wisp of gratitude or loyalty. You do not buy loyalty by letting clients violate your credit terms.

Increase Cash Flow by Increasing Sales

Most entrepreneurs would argue that increasing sales is the first step to increasing cash flow. But sales alone aren't the answer. Driving up sales without a thorough approach to cash flow and profit management will wind up enriching everybody but you. You'll need more people, more equipment, more inventory, more freight, more postage, etc., and everybody will get richer—but will you?

Sometimes it's even helpful to cut back sales volume, cut out the least profitable product lines or parts of a business, and alter the economics for the better—much like pruning a bush so it can grow straighter and stronger.

However, having said that, it is still probably your goal to make your business bigger, and that's fine. But remember there are usually more opportunities than there are resources, so choose those that provide the best margins and the best cash flow, not those that provide tightest margins and worst cash flow. In other words, grow sales *strategically.*

I once consulted with a manufacturer who was enjoying sales growth of more than 25% per calendar quarter but was so strapped for cash he was a walking ulcer. More than 80% of his sales were to three big chain store accounts, who routinely took 90 to 120 days to pay. He was about to get his product line into a fourth comparable chain when I insisted he slam on the brakes.

A year later, the business had again doubled, but the percentage in the chains was cut in half as he focused on distribution to a lot of small independents who paid net 30 or in advance, and on private-label manufacturing, for which he got paid 50% in advance.

I do like to see capital created rather than borrowed.

The story of my friend the late George Douglas exemplifies this kind of unique resourcefulness. George went broke in a big way in a direct-sales business and wound up sitting in his bare house, all the furniture gone, and nothing left but a box of 48 copies of the book *Think and Grow Rich* and a dozen broken down auto-dialing (telephone marketing) computers. George had used these machines to set up appointments for his salespeople in his now-defunct business. He knew they could work, and he believed in them. He used the books in his classes to motivate his salespeople.

George asked himself what resources he could draw on to get some cash. He repaired the auto-dialers so they could be sold as used but operable equipment. Then he got on the phone, calling insurance salespeople, real estate agents, and other salespeople, inviting them to a free seminar on using auto-dialers to increase business. He offered a free copy of *Think and Grow Rich* to anybody who came to the meeting.

He called and invited hundreds. About a dozen salespeople showed up. He nervously stood up in front of the group, explained how auto-dialers work, how he used them successfully, and how he helped others use them. Then he gave a demonstration and offered a unique "rent-and-try-then-buy" offer on the machines he had in stock. That evening, George sold eight machines; in the first month he collected $800.00 for rentals. He discovered that he had a knack for selling this type of equipment.

In short order, he found a manufacturer of auto-dialers and convinced him to sell the machines at wholesale as George needed them, without an inventory requirement, franchise fee, or other up-front payment. In the next few years, he built a large business, with national advertising and sales representatives selling these machines. He also used some of the profits from that business to invest in a new idea for computer software, and that, too, turned into a very successful business. He went from bankruptcy to big money without borrowing a nickel.

Only a few years later, he was grooming replacements to run his companies, personally working two weeks a month, and sailing the Caribbean on his yacht the other two weeks of the month.

Contrast this with the dotcommers who blew through millions and millions of dollars of capital without even coming close to making one honest dollar.

One of the key principles I talk about in my Renegade Millionaire seminars is that Renegade Millionaires are resourceful, not necessarily full of resources.

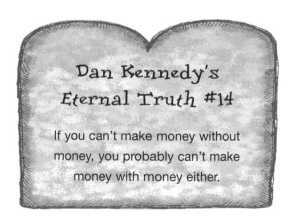

Dan Kennedy's
Eternal Truth #14

If you can't make money without money, you probably can't make money with money either.

Find or Invent a "Slack Adjuster"

Those in the used-car business use the term *slack adjuster* to describe the occasional great buy they find somewhere, like a ten-year-old car in mint condition that they buy for $500.00 and can sell for $2,000.00, a 400% markup, far exceeding their normal markup.

A slack adjuster is something you sell that gives you a surge of extra profit to help pick up the slack.

In the appliance business, it's the add-on warranties. In the finance business, it's "credit life insurance"—probably the worst insurance buy ever perpetrated on consumers.

One of my members owns a couple of neighborhood hardware stores. Two years ago, he added Grille Shops, in which he sells all kinds of barbeque grills, including the incredibly expensive, elaborate "built-in" gas grills. He only sells two or three of the $5,000.00 to $7,000.00 grill installations a season, but they pick up the slack for a lot of $3.00 hammers.

Two Commonly Underutilized Means of Boosting Sales, Profits, and Cash Flow

Well-run, sophisticated direct marketing/mail-order companies do two things well that a lot of other businesses miss altogether.

One is the instant upsell.

If you call and order from a catalog company, the person taking the order will usually end the call by asking you to consider one or more special offers of the day. If you call and order after seeing a TV infomercial, the person taking the order may offer you a second of the same item you're buying at half price or offer you a chance to buy an unrelated, extra item. In most of these cases, from 5% to as high as 20% of the customers say yes to one of these upsells. It costs a lot less to get the upsell than to get the person calling in to buy the first item; you're only adding minutes on the phone, not pages to a catalog or commercial time on TV.

Some smart businesspeople "get this," and incorporate it into their operations one way or another. One restaurant chain lists a recommended wine along with each entrée on its menu and pays bonuses to its waitstaff who sell its premium desserts. In movie theaters, you are "bumped up" from regular size to jumbo size beverages and popcorn tubs because "it's only x cents more"— but those x cents provide a much higher profit margin than the core purchase.

Another way to think about this: by failing to devise and use upsells, you leave 5% to 20% of the money readily available to you for the asking safely inside your customers' wallets instead of in your cash register where it rightfully belongs!

The other neglected opportunity is cross-selling. One chain of gourmet food shops has a checklist at each cash register so if a customer is buying any kind of sausage without cheese, the clerk suggests a cheese; or if the customer is buying a cheese without a sausage, vice versa. A chain of menswear stores carefully tracks customers who've bought suits and ties but no sportswear and sends them sportswear offers and coupons. Customers who have bought sportswear but no suits get offers and coupons for suits.

My coaching member Chet Rowland, who owns Florida's most successful pest control company, is a master at cross-selling. He aggressively markets termite protection to his customers who are regular monthly pest control. Customers who answer his ads for termite protection are then sold monthly pest control. And so on. In his business, there is a matrix of eight different cross-selling situations.

Pursuing these opportunities not only increases sales but produces profitable sales and improved cash flow because you are leveraging the same customers, not having to invest in acquiring new ones.

The Ultimate MCF Tactic: "Prepay"

The fastest way to multiply cash flow is to get customers to pay in advance for goods and/or services to be delivered later, preferably over time.

When I took over a very troubled, negative cash-flow manufacturing company, we immediately instituted a 5% prepay discount on repeat orders, 7% on new orders. Nearly 20% of our accounts switched to paying in advance, and it made a huge difference.

Pre-paid "memberships" have been devised and successfully sold by members or clients of mine who are chiropractors or owners of martial arts schools, restaurants, clothing stores, and many other kinds of businesses. One photography studio owner I know sells five-, seven-, and ten-year prepaid family portrait plans. The most expensive of which is about $30,000.00 in services and products if purchased piecemeal, but it is discounted to $19,000.00 prepaid. He says he usually sells only one, sometimes two of these plans per month, but over the past four years, he's used these big chunks of money to first pay off some high-interest credit cards, then pay cash for new equipment, and finally to invest in income-producing real estate.

Far too many would-be entrepreneurs are stopped in their tracks by lack of capital, when ingenuity would serve as a perfectly satisfactory substitute.

The most interesting entrepreneurs to me are the ones who create their own capital from sales. I got to know Bob Stupak, who built the Vegas World Hotel and Casino (now The Stratosphere) from the ground up, paying for construction on each floor as money came in from his sale of prepaid vacation packages. He turned an intangible into a tangible product that could be sold and collected for in advance of its use and used it to build the hotel itself—without a dime of debt in construction loans. (You'll find a copy of his original ad, incidentally, in my book *The Ultimate Marketing Plan*.)

Through some or all of these methods you can multiply and maximize your business's cash flow, and as a result, give yourself every possible opportunity to win big.

CHAPTER 12

How to Achieve
Peak Productivity

The hurrieder I go, the behinder I get.

—PENNSYLVANIA DUTCH SAYING

A s a teenager, I worked summers as a groom at a harness racetrack, taking care of horses and shoveling manure. A lot of manure. Every workday started at 5:00 A.M., stopped around 1:00 P.M., started back up about 5:00 P.M. to get the horses that were racing that night ready, and finished after the races, 10:00 or 11:00 P.M.

During the day, I worked in aluminum-roofed barns that absorbed the sun's heat and cooked us pretty well. I filled wicker baskets with manure, about two per stall from three to a dozen stalls, hauled the baskets the length of the barn, hoisted them up, and emptied them into the manure wagons. I fed, watered, and groomed the horses. I worked on their sore legs and feet. I walked them. I stacked bales of straw and hay.

All of it was hard work. Looking back, I have fondness and nostalgia for it all. So much so, I've returned and now own about two dozen racehorses, even drive some in races at a major racetrack. But I do not shovel the manure. I'm not *that* nostalgic.

But no matter how hard you have worked in previous jobs, you'll discover that running your business is even harder, more intense work. The pace and pressure of being the person in charge is unlike any other, and it requires masterful organization, control, and use of time. It requires that you have the ability to do many things at once. The multiple demands on the entrepreneur's time are extraordinary, and you need extraordinary measures to match these demands.

Time is the most valuable asset any entrepreneur possesses. Time to step aside and think. Time to network. Time to solve

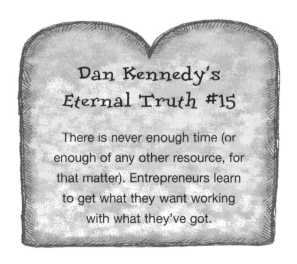

Dan Kennedy's Eternal Truth #15

There is never enough time (or enough of any other resource, for that matter). Entrepreneurs learn to get what they want working with what they've got.

problems. Time to invent sales and marketing breakthroughs. *The use or misuse of your time*—the degree with which you achieve peak productivity—will determine your success as an entrepreneur.

Time may be the biggest problem in business, and the biggest societal concern of the moment. The *Fortune* 500 companies spend millions annually on time management training and productivity analysis. The market is clogged with time management systems and seminars. Despite all this, most businesspeople I know are still woefully disorganized, behind in their work, running faster and faster to try to catch up. One research study I read about some years ago concluded that the average corporate CEO actually logs less than 90 minutes a day of genuinely productive time. Lee Iacocca told me he doubted it was that much! And I suggest entrepreneurs have even bigger problems with time than do corporate executives.

Imagine—in an eight to ten hour workday, being able to count just 90 minutes of it as productive! Clearly, you can give yourself a tremendous competitive advantage if you can make more of your time productive.

Why Is Time Such a Problem?

To achieve peak productivity, you've got to know what it is, when you're hitting it, and when you're not. Most people have no clue. Most people work harder and faster without the ability to determine whether they're really getting anywhere.

I have devoted quite a bit of thought to defining what productivity really is—and what it isn't. I've developed this definition:

Peak productivity is the use of your time, energy, intelligence, resources, and opportunities in a manner calculated to move you measurably closer to meaningful goals.

Once you understand and accept this definition, you'll be better able to choose what to do, what to delegate, and what to leave undone.

Why "Do It Now" May Not Be the Best Advice

The favorite affirmation of the late self-made multimillionaire and success expert W. Clement Stone is "Do it now!" Given that something should be done and should be done by you, then "Do it now!" is good advice. Procrastination is insidious.

But many people erroneously accept the do-it-now idea as a prison sentence requiring them to try and do *everything* **now. Some things shouldn't be done now**. Some things should be deliberately assigned to next week or next month. Some things shouldn't be done at all. And the busier I am and the older I get, the more I conclude that the greatest wisdom of all is in astutely choosing what *not* to do.

It's interesting how obligated most people feel to answer a ringing phone. They'll interrupt whatever they are doing to pick up the receiver, even if they are in the shower! When somebody calls the office and leaves a message, people feel obligated to call back, even when they don't know the caller! Now, with cell phones, people put themselves "on point" 24-7, without even a moment's peace. In fact, I'm lately seeing men in airport restrooms, standing at urinals, peeing, and talking on their cell phones. Sad and pathetic. If you can't even pee in peace, you're not Mr. Important; you're Mr. Idiot.

The same is true for faxes and e-mails and correspondence. When people receive these in the office, they feel obligated to reply, quickly. Because someone appears in the office doorway,

It bewilders a lot of people that I, for example, will go days without checking my phone messages or opening my mail. And at home, I'll often take the phone off the hook for hours to write, nap, watch a game, whatever. "Having that phone off the hook would drive me crazy," a friend said. "I'd be worrying the whole time about who might be trying to call me."

For some years, I have refused to take any unscheduled business calls, and I operate entirely by clustered phone appointments. I do not own a cell phone, and I will not use e-mail. For a time, I was mocked, but of late, a number of famous CEOs are stating they've disconnected their e-mail. Even one of the top Internet marketing consultants in America refuses to use it personally!

they feel obligated to acknowledge them, to invite them in, to talk with them. And on and on.

You have to shake off the shackles of ordinary and customary obligations and feel free to do whatever assists you in achieving peak productivity.

I deal with this in much greater detail—and prove to you with examples that you can still control access to you, your time, and your life in ANY business—in my book *No B.S. Time Management.* One very important reason you should get and read this book is to learn techniques you can use to work interruption-free, to better organize, prioritize, and stick to your highest value responsibilities and opportunities.

The Yes or No Test

These days, when someone asks me to do something, attend a meeting, talk with somebody, read something, whatever, I silently ask myself: *Is this going to move me measurably closer to a goal?* If not, I do my best to say no.

I think in terms of *investing* time. After all, if time is money, then you must either be spending or investing it. Would you knowingly invest your money in, say, a stock that promised no gain or dividends? No. You might choose to spend some money on things offering no monetary profit such as tickets to the theater, flowers for your spouse, or a vacation. But investing time in activities unlikely to pay any kind of dividend is stupid. You must be very astute at making these time-investment decisions.

So, always ask yourself, is this demand on my time a wise investment? Yes or no?

What Now?

One of the classic problems faced by new entrepreneurs is the absence of an imposed work plan. As someone else's employee, a work plan is imposed on you by your employer. Your adherence to that plan may be policed by managers and supervisors. You are held accountable for effectiveness in adhering to and accomplishing that plan. Deviations from the imposed plan are restricted, sometimes punished. That imposed plan causes you to behave in a disciplined fashion. For example, you get up at a certain time every morning to arrive at work at a set, acceptable time. Maybe you get all your expense reports in order every Thursday afternoon because you are expected to submit them on Friday. You get your monthly newsletter out to your customers because that's part of the imposed plan.

Now you're an entrepreneur. You are your own boss—you can smash that alarm clock with a sledgehammer and set your own hours. You decide what will be done, when, and how.

But for many new entrepreneurs, when they get free of the job, they don't know what to do next. It's too much freedom. They wind up paralyzed, looking around for somebody to tell them what to do.

You have to set up your own work plan. I am most productive when I operate under a self-imposed work plan that creates as much discipline as any employer-imposed plan would—preferably more. You have to be tough on yourself and set deadlines. If you wouldn't accept an excuse from someone working for you, you can't accept it from yourself. If you're trying to set an example of leadership for others around you, you have to overdo it: be more organized and more punctual than they need to be.

Last year, I wrote two books for bookstore distribution, four other books for mail-order distribution, and several audio programs. I edited two monthly newsletters and did direct-response copywriting for clients. If I wrote only when I felt like it, when I was inspired, when the time was right, I'd be finishing last year's workload in my next life. No, I wrote when I was tired, when I was uninspired, when I was too busy, not just in my office but on airplanes and in hotel rooms. I put myself under self-imposed work plans and deadlines to create discipline.

My friend John Carlton, a top direct-response copywriter, says the greatest of all inventions in all of recorded history is the deadline. Without it, nothing else would ever have gotten done with any of the other inventions.

Nobody's going to do this for you. You're on your own. You must impose deadlines on yourself.

Refuse to Let Them Steal Your Time

Another prevalent problem entrepreneurs fight in achieving peak productivity is other people's disrespect for time. Most people don't value their time very highly, and as a result, don't place much value on yours either. Given half a chance, most people will waste your time.

I am militant about guarding my time. I learned, for example, not to set up business meetings in restaurants. If I was going to a business lunch with someone, I'd have them first come to my office. When you arrange to meet people in restaurants, you waste a lot of time waiting for them because very few people are punctual. If they're late coming to your office, productivity can continue until they arrive.

Back when I was in my office most days, I had all my incoming calls very carefully screened. This did occasionally irritate people, but that only served notice to me that the irritated person was not a very successful businessperson. He may be able to afford to waste time; I can't. So in my office, no calls were put through nor were any messages even accepted unless the caller fully identified himself and the reasons for calling. My best guess is that there were a dozen callers a day who did not get through to me and never did because they refused to identify themselves. Even at just three minutes a call, that alone saved me 36 minutes a day and give or take, 900 minutes a year.

Now my screening methods are even more stringent.

My assistant encourages people to send or fax me brief, introductory notes before trying to get on the phone with me. Many times, she can handle these matters, and I'm not needed at all.

Put a Stake Through the Heart of Every "Time Vampire" Who Comes Your Way

"Time vampires" are people dedicated to sucking up your time. In the process, they also suck out a lot of your energy, leaving you white, weak, and behind schedule. These are the repctitive, frequent drop-in visitors. Or these could be an employee whose favorite phrase is, "Have you got a minute?" Or one who is infected with "meeting-itis." They're chronically disorganized. Each time one of these vampires drops by and hangs out, picture him or her sinking teeth into your neck and sucking out a pint or two.

Suppose, for example, you want to make $100,000.00 this year, which means your work hour is worth about $36.00, which is about 60 cents a minute. So when a time vampire sucks up 20 minutes in a meeting for something that could have been handled with a four-minute phone call, that person just sucked more than $9.00 right out of your wallet. If that happens five times in a week, you lose $45.00. Over 50 weeks, that's $2,250.00. If you have ten of these vampires hanging around, you're down $22,500.00 before you get out of the starting gate toward the $100,000.00 goal. That's nearly a 25% weight handicap, too much to overcome.

The Secrets of Secrets of Getting Rich

Perhaps you think I'm overdoing this—beating this drum too loudly. But let me tell you why it's impossible to overemphasize the deliberate achievement of peak productivity. It is the *secret of secrets* to getting rich.

Exceptional success in any business is the result of strategically directing ever-increasing amounts of your time to the activities you're very good at and very excited about, to the highest value responsibilities, to only the best opportunities. When you start a business, you do it all. The trick is to stay at that stage as briefly as possible and to grow out of it by directing increasing amounts of your time to those aspects of the business you have the most passion for and do best.

You can never make this happen if your time is being abused, wasted, lost, sucked up by vampires, and controlled by everybody but you.

CHAPTER 13

How Entrepreneurs
Attract Good Luck

The more we know about what we really want,
the better prepared we are to recognize
favorable chances and extract good luck.

—A. H. Z. CARR, *HOW TO ATTRACT GOOD LUCK*

I t's very common for authors of business and success books to insist that there's no such thing as luck. This is not true. There is, quite obviously, luck. People do "get discovered." Coincidences do turn to gain. For example, who I sit by in an airplane is the luck of the draw, yet, a number of times, conversations with those people have turned into business, opportunity, and income for me. Sure, I took the initiative to steer the conversation in productive directions, I was mentally prepared, and I was in the airplane, but, still, the luck of the draw put the right person beside me.

So I believe in luck, I believe we get lucky breaks, and I don't think there's anything wrong with looking for a little luck and acknowledging it when we get it. On the other hand, let's remember that the lucky rabbit's foot sure didn't bring much luck to that rabbit.

Most entrepreneurs I deal with share a belief and cheerful expectation in luck and try to do their part to facilitate it. They and I believe that people can learn to take certain actions that will, in effect, make them lucky.

A book summarizing a lot of scientific research done about "lucky people" is *The Luck Factor* by Dr. Richard Wiseman. It provides evidence that you can actually increase the good luck in your life, on purpose.

Using Your Subconscious Mind

The biggest secret to deliberately making yourself lucky does not come as a set of concrete instructions—it has more to do with your subconscious mind. There just aren't enough pages in this book to convince you of the awesome power of your subconscious mind or how it works. I can only urge you to study it on your own. You might want to begin with the book *The New Psycho-Cybernetics* by Dr. Maxwell Maltz and me. (You can get more information at www.psycho-cybernetics.com.)

I have thoroughly satisfied myself that the subconscious mind can be programmed or directed to search its vast stores to select, compile, and provide appropriate information and then give you the "flash of inspiration" you need to solve a nagging problem, go to the right place at the right time, say the right thing, or do the right thing. This is a computer-like function, and most people can accept it as logical and true, even if they don't make a practice of using it. It's certainly nothing new; Thomas Edison used to lock himself in a quiet room, give commands to his subconscious mind, and, as he described it, "sit for ideas."

But the properly programmed and energized subconscious mind can go much farther than that. Many very successful entrepreneurs, some scientists, and some psychologists believe that it can actually reach out and get needed information from the combined intelligence of the universe and that it can set up a magnetic field that actually attracts the people, resources, and ideas needed to accomplish a particular goal.

Define Your Purpose

The programming tool for unleashing the full powers of your subconscious mind is definition of purpose. The clearer your picture of what you want, the more activity you inspire inside your subconscious system. There are three main ways to put this to work, and they all involve writing.

1. *Continually develop your goals in writing.* Paul Meyer, founder of the Success Motivation Institute, says, "If you are not making the progress you'd like to make, it is probably because your goals are not clearly defined." There is power in continually sharpening the definition of your goals on paper. Clarity *is* power.

2. *Write out your business plan.* A written, detailed business plan combines goal setting, action planning, and problem solving. It makes ideas believable.

3. *Create and use daily checklists.* You would never want to be on an airplane where the crew had reviewed the preflight processes by memory rather than by referring to checklists. Isn't your day and your use of your time equally important?

These three action steps have great practical value, but they also serve to communicate to your subconscious mind, in an organized manner, the seriousness of your objectives. Then wonderful things happen!

How to Be in the Right Place at the Right Time

Some years ago, I was navigating a troubled company through a turnaround and, fortunately, using all three of these action tools to the best of my ability. I put trust in my subconscious system (largely because there wasn't anything else around to trust) and, from time to time, got some very valuable "flashes."

For some time, I'd been thinking about the possibility of selling off part of the company's business in order to get new capital to strengthen the remaining business. One afternoon, a "flash" crystallized that for me; a plan came into my thoughts out of nowhere, to sell the manufacturing part of the company to a competitor in that arena, then use that capital to make the retail marketing part of the company stronger. It was all so clear in my mind that at that moment, I picked up the phone and called the competing company's president and asked for an appointment to fly into his city and meet with him to discuss a business proposition. The next day, I described my proposal—with no preparation, just as it came to me—and immediately came to an agreement in principle. In just one week, the details were worked out, contracts signed, and an unprofitable part of my company's business was converted to a six-figure sum.

I later learned that I had selected the perfect time to approach this competitor. The president was right in the midst of deciding whether to more aggressively pursue additional business in the particular market in which we were competing or to abandon that market and pursue expansion opportunities elsewhere. Had I been even a week later with my call, decisions would already have been made, possibly making our deal unworkable. Had I been a month or two earlier, the president would not have been ready. My timing was perfect. A lucky break?

No. "Luck" like this is a result of having clearly defined goals, working hard, associating with people who could facilitate success, being involved in situations where opportunities can arise, and continuing personal education and improvement. Oh, and *doing* something.

To have good fortune, you have to do enough to help the pendulum swing in your direction. Quarterbacks that complete a lot of passes and throw a lot of touchdown passes throw a bunch of interceptions, too. Babe Ruth had more strikeouts than home runs. Edison had a warehouse full of failed, abandoned experiments. Just about every successful entrepreneur I know

Dan Kennedy's
Eternal Truth #16

Even a blind hog finds a truffle
once in a while—as long as
it keeps poking around.

I frequently create ad campaigns and direct-mail campaigns that bring in millions of dollars for my clients or that outperform their prior campaigns by impressive margins. I've heard people commenting how "lucky" I am to have this "knack." Nobody mentions the other campaigns I do every year that get results ranging from mediocre to nonexistent. (To be fair, I don't either!) But this sort of thing is neither knack nor luck; it is work.

More importantly, it is like drilling multiple oil wells to hit one gusher.

tries a lot of ideas every year and profits handsomely if only one or two succeed. One of my best clients tested six different "brilliant ideas" for doing more business with his past customers last year. Five of these ideas flopped. The sixth has turned into a million-dollar-a-year money machine. My very successful *No B.S. Marketing Letter* is what everybody sees now. Few know it was preceded by my creating and publishing four different, much less successful newsletters and a magazine, all abandoned.

Luck Is a Product of Universal Law

There are certain universal laws. Gravity, for example, works the same way every time, in every situation, for every one of us, whether we know about it or are ignorant of it, whether we think about it or not, whether we believe it or not. Drop ten pencils, all ten fall to the ground.

Some other laws aren't so easily proven. My friend the late Foster Hibbard taught that the more you give, the more you get. I've found that the more you give, the more "luck" you get. I now use and teach Foster Hibbard's method for implementing this idea: you establish "the habit of giving" by opening up a separate, dedicated bank account, your "giving account." Into it you deposit 1% to 10% of the money that comes to you from any and every source and give that money away as you see fit, with no strings attached.

I'm here to tell you that giving away money this way is a fast path to wealth. It energizes the subconscious mind with a wealth and success consciousness unlike anything you've ever experienced.

I confess this was a very difficult idea for me to buy into. It's illogical. If you have $2 and give away $1, you've got $1 left. You haven't increased your wealth, you've decreased it, right? Wrong. When I first started this, I couldn't afford it. I didn't have any extra money. But I decided to test it, and I have now proven it works.

Let me say, though, that this works only when you strictly follow all the rules. You set up the account. You commit to a percentage. You put that percentage into your giving account every time you get money—no exceptions, no excuses. You give it away with no expectation of return. Try it, for a couple of months and stay open to real serendipity and to new financial gain coming at you from the most unexpected sources.

Some Practical Advice on Attracting Good Luck

Keep an open mind and get a lot of exposure. You are sure to attract good luck this way. It's a big mistake to get myopic. Many businesspeople have tunnel vision, and as a result, they cut themselves off from opportunity altogether. Breakthrough ideas usually come from unusual sources, but if the clothing store owner spends all day, every day in the store, only stepping out to trade association meetings and conventions, he is letting luck come in through one very tiny hole. From businesspeople like this, you'll hear things like, "We've never done it that way before . . . . That may be OK there, but not in our business." They close their minds and shut themselves off from the world.

Drive to your store or office by different routes. Every month, pick a magazine off the newsstand you've never read before and read it. Make a point of talking to cab drivers, restaurant servers, and others you might not normally strike up a conversation with. Give yourself little bits of exposure to ideas, experiences, and people outside the normal, narrow scope of your business and see what happens. Something will.

CHAPTER 14

Staying Sane in
an Insane World

By night an atheist half believes in God.

—EDWARD YOUNG

This is a rather "personal" chapter.

I've had an enormous amount of success and good fortune in my life, and I am very grateful. At the moment I am writing these lines, I am thoroughly enjoying my life, more so than at any prior time, and I am, with good reason, more optimistic about what's around the next corner than I have ever been.

I've also had a pretty large helping of stress, failure, disappointment, pain, and tragedy in my life. Because—as I teach and insist—all news is good news, it has all led somewhere beneficial. But that does not mean I'd wish the experiences on anybody.

In 2002, I was divorced, and I imagine just like everybody else going through that, I questioned my behavior, even my entire life. I wished I'd spent more time with my stepdaughter, who I love deeply. As my wife was also my business partner, I had the stressful need to make dramatic changes far faster than I'd planned. In 2003, I lost my father, and I imagine like most sons, questioned if I had done enough. Should I have been there more? Heck, this was just one 12-month calendar. No need to bore you with the entire history.

As I said, this is a personal chapter even more so than the others in this book, written in the hope something said here, even if painful to say, might be of special help to somebody. You can B.S. by omission just as by statement, and I promised a no B.S. book.

Danger Ahead

The danger for the entrepreneur is to become totally absorbed in the success of the business to the detriment of all other parts of life. There are certainly times and circumstances when you must make your business your number-one priority, but there are also risks attached. If you let your business become the only priority and become everything in your life, look out! Investing all your identity and self-esteem in a business takes away your opportunity to operate objectively and to change directions in your life as you learn, grow, and change.

How to Be a Business Success and Have It Not Matter

In 1992, I was having my all-time, best-ever year in business. But one day I arrived home from my business trip to be told by my wife that she was leaving me. We later reconciled, but let me tell you, as the full impact of that evening set in, the fact that I was at

Dan Kennedy's
Eternal Truth #17

No one on his deathbed says,
"I wish I'd spent more time
at the office."
Not even a true entrepreneur.

the peak of success in my career became remarkably unimportant and unsatisfying.

In 2002, as I said, my wife and I divorced after 22 years of marriage. Such things are never one-sided, and there's opportunity here to play he said/she said, he did/she did, he didn't/she didn't. I admit, I wonder if I'd have been better off had we not reconciled in 1993. The temptation is to say yes; the reality may be no. In any case, the 2002 events were tumultuous, disturbing, depressing, and of course life-changing. And they have once again caused me to re-examine priorities, although I was already well on my way and perfectly in sync with a planned and written schedule to sharply curtail my business activities. I had already slashed business travel by 70% , sold one business, and made other changes.

I recognize that it must be very difficult to be married to a very ambitious entrepreneur. Then again, it may not be a breezy walk in the park being married to a fixed-wage 9-to-5'er either. Just different. I truthfully haven't drawn many lessons from my

You will never hear me dispense much marriage advice. Although, to be fair, one of the most published, most publicized, best known authors of relationship, love and marriage advice books has been divorced five times, one of those from another relationship expert and best-selling author on these same subjects. Apparently, she was actually from Venus, he from Mars. *Sex and the City* actress Kim Cattrell, who wrote an entire how-to book on sexual satisfaction, is now divorced from the husband who was the book's co-author. Her complaint: all he was interested in was sex. If these are the experts, I guess I could wade in.

22 years of marriage and divorce about what to do differently. But I have resolved to try to choose more cautiously and appropriately if I get one more shot.

All these events in my life led to the hope that a person can have different, but equally important, priorities in life. That you do not have to have a simple, vertical ladder with only one item on each rung. That there are other ways to manage all the aspects of life. For me, business activities are fun and financial success is important. So business *is* a top priority, and I can't deny that. But so are my important relationships, my health, my hobby. Can you have four different number-one items?

What I would say, as advice, is brief: if you feel secure in your marriage or significant-other relationship, I hope you're right, but I wouldn't bet money on it. The busy entrepreneur's tendency is not to go looking for trouble—after all, you've got enough of that finding you every single day without probing for it. As a natural result, squeakiest wheels do get grease, anything short of crises get procrastination. I would now say, you do need to look for trouble in your relationship and make sure there isn't any, early and often.

Success in isolation is not success at all. You probably won't get a chance to deal with your life priorities in orderly sequence: first, master a business; second, get rich; third, create relationships; fourth, turn attention to health, etc. Thus, the greatest challenge of living as an entrepreneur is doing many things simultaneously, few sequentially.

Several years ago, via flunking an insurance physical, I was diagnosed diabetic. As there's no known family history, I'm chalking it up to a combination of damage to the pancreas from heavy drinking in my early adult life (I no longer drink), years of eating poorly, especially while maintaining a grueling travel schedule, and letting my weight reach and hover at 245.

For now, I've brought the diabetes under satisfactory control without insulin with a very demanding regimen of carb-controlled eating, a complex array of nutritional supplements (more than 40 pills per day), and moderate exercise. I brought my weight to 205 and have kept it there. But this is no fun. It's time-consuming and over time is likely only to delay inevitable complications, not prevent them.

I've done so much work in the area of diet and nutrition, and been so frustrated and amazed at the truly terrible health advice proliferate in the marketplace, I've been toying with doing something about it. If I do, you'll find it happening at www.damnthe

Incidentally, many years ago, for consecutive years, I was hitting the booze morning, noon, night, drinking to blackout. I have huge blanks in memory from that time. I have my share of funny stories; all drunks do. I got very good at hiding the problem and functioning with it. None of this is important at all, unless you have a drinking problem and are denying it or "managing" it or procrastinating about doing something about it. Every day you do, the cumulative damage to your health, probably to your marriage, maybe to your business, is incalculable and largely irreversible. I quit cold turkey. No big hit-bottom, turning-point story either—at least I can't remember it. But I just quit.

Now, years later, I can have a beer or drink with no urge for a second, no adverse occurrences. Most years, I have one on my birthday, one on New Year's Eve, and about half a beer once during the summer. There are differences of opinion about alcoholism. Some experts would say I could never have been an alcoholic or I could not now even taste without escalating use. I don't know if that's true or not. I don't claim clinical expertise, only firsthand experience.

Here is what I would say: if you can quit, quit. If you can't, get help and quit. Now. We all think we can control our addictions. Doctors become addicted to drugs they dispense to themselves, insisting they know enough to avoid addiction. They are always proven wrong, often with disastrous consequences. I once had someone working for me who thought he could just be a weekend recreational cocaine user. He was wrong. Because you are entrepreneurial, it is natural to believe you can do anything, handle anything, and very unnatural to admit to yourself—let alone anyone else—that you can't.

I have very few regrets in life. I could provide a list nearly as long as this book of things I might do differently, but few rise to the level of regret. One, though, is that I regret not quitting drinking years before I did.

The first letter I ever got about this was from a businessman in Canada who, as a result of similar remarks he heard from me at a seminar, quit drinking, turned around a troubled business, fixed an estranged marriage, and, in many ways, dramatically improved his life. His letter alone made saying these things worth it. Over the years since, I've gotten more than 50 similar letters from people motivated to confront their damaging addictions thanks to my personal disclosures. If I happen to be talking to you right now, please do something. Denial is a lousy strategy.

doctors.com. Once again, it's damnably hard to cage the entrepreneurial urges.

Anyway, my advice about this is basic: now, not later. Financial success achieved at the price of ill health that could have been prevented, a mistake.

Anyway, I have more than one "top priority." These days, rather than giving one of the four priorities the top rung to itself, I'm doing my level best to give each a share of every single day. I'll let you know how that plan works out!

Integrity Is Strategy

It is often easier to create temporary success if you ignore the issue of integrity. It may be tempting to rig product demonstrations, make false advertising claims, or cheat in other ways, but sooner or later, you're going to get caught—if not by the law, by unsatisfied customers.

Call it what you wish—karma, universal law, reciprocity, whatever—but what goes around does seem to come around. So the big question is, can you be a "nice guy" and a success in business, too? Well, I don't know if I'd want to pit the late Mother Teresa against Donald Trump in a negotiation, but that doesn't mean you have to operate without integrity to do well as an entrepreneur.

Integrity has become hot marketing strategy. There are three basic categories of ethical standards in relationships between business and customers. Figure 14.1 illustrates these standards.

FIGURE **14.1:** Ethical Continuum

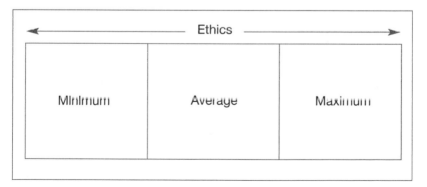

Dan Kennedy's
Eternal Truth #18

What goes around,
comes around.

Minimum Ethics

We will do just enough to comply with all laws, stay out of jail, and deter lawsuits or returns for refunds.

Several years ago, at a seminar, on a dare, I made a list of ten well-known companies in diverse industries, all viewed as financially healthy at the time. I predicted they would be bankrupt within two years. My list was made up of businesses I believed were operating via this minimum standard. Two years later, seven of the ten were bankrupt, and an eighth had been acquired while on the verge of bankruptcy. Just recently, one of the two remaining companies who beat my prediction announced first-quarter losses of $130 million and massive layoffs.

Average Ethics

We will give the customer fair exchange, reasonable value for their dollars—no, less but no more. Most businesses operate at this stage. As a result, during good times, they'll get average results, turn a profit, and stay in business.

Maximum Ethics

We will not ask just how we can get more sales, we will ask how we can give more and better service. We will strive to amaze and astound customers with far "more" and "better" than they expect.

Why Shoot for Maximum Ethics

The entrepreneur who constantly strives to be of greater and better service to his or her clientele has the edge in good times or bad. The entrepreneur constantly striving to better reward customers for their patronage is on ethical high ground and will be amply rewarded—providing, of course, he also works, markets, promotes, sells, and manages wisely.

There are many good reasons for maximum ethical standards and behavior in business. Peace of mind is one of them. Depending on spiritual beliefs, your seating assignment in the afterlife might be another. If no other reason motivates you, you might consider its value as plain, simple, good business.

I don't think you need morality to operate ethically. Practical considerations alone are sufficient motivation.

On the other hand, let's be careful not to confuse integrity with either timidity or guilt. I deal with a lot of entrepreneurs sabotaged by their own negative and guilty attitudes about doing well. They underprice their goods and services, they underpromise in their advertising.

How to Develop and Profit from the Power of Faith

I've appeared as a speaker on events with the Reverend Robert Schuller a number of times. Schuller often challenges people with the provocative question, "What plans would you have on your drawing board if you knew you could not fail?" Wouldn't it be wonderful to approach your daily activities with that kind of confidence? Well, you can. It is just an act of faith.

Personal faith is not usually a topic entrepreneurs discuss openly, but just about every highly successful person I've ever known has a very definite set of spiritual beliefs and, as a result, acts with faith.

For me, faith is based on four simple ideas:

1. There is plan and purpose behind our lives.
2. We're here to learn some things and to accomplish some things.
3. We were intended and are invited to live prosperously.
4. When operating within certain parameters, we have every reason to expect positive results.

This solid expectation of positive results empowers you to cut through the clutter and confusion of self-doubt, fear, criticism, cynicism, negativism, and other obstacles.

For me, the parameters include the pursuit of goals that can be achieved by enriching others, not at the expense of others; accepting responsibility for my actions; and the pursuit of the purpose to which all goals relate. These are certainly not the only parameters for faith. Yours may very well differ from mine. It's not my purpose here to impose my spiritual beliefs on you or anybody else. But I feel that I would have presented an incomplete picture of what I've found necessary for entrepreneurial success without discussing this.

Lee Iacocca has written that you have to collect and evaluate accurate research data and other information in order to make good business decisions. He then says that, no matter how much information you get, it's never enough to guarantee the decision, and at some point you have to "take the leap of faith."

Entrepreneurs Need Extraordinary Faith in This Crazy World

Is change more rapid and unpredictable than ever? It certainly seems that way. Globally, old enemies disappear or become new friends; old friends become new enemies. Who's who and what's what is uncertain and confusing. Governments are getting closer to having to pay the piper for mounting mammoth deficits, and nobody can be sure how that price will be extracted from our hides. In business, old industries die, new industries are invented. Old reliable advertising methods fail, new tools emerge. The rules change daily, it seems. Competition is faster, smarter, tougher.

Ray Kroc made an interesting statement of faith in a TV interview some years ago when asked if he was ever irritated at how quickly his competitors copied everything McDonald's did. "Not at all," he replied. "We invent faster than they can copy."

That's what entrepreneurship's all about—confidently inventing new products, services, processes, solutions. And the secret to sanity, even under intense pressure, even when confronted by confusing crisis, is to *act with faith*. It is that simple; take action.

Once, shortly after taking over a very troubled company, during a particularly difficult day, the corporation's comptroller brought more bad news to my office: our most important, essential supplier had called and cut us off. Our company owed this vendor a large sum of money for past-due invoices, and the vendor refused to ship the current order, which we needed desperately. There wasn't a dime in the checking account to give him.

What would you do?

I got on the first available plane to Minneapolis and was parked on that vendor's doorstep when the president arrived the next morning. We sat down face to face, and we worked out an agreement.

That "action model" has served me very well many times in my business career.

CHAPTER 15

Why and How to Build
Your Own Mini
Conglomerate

It's an impossible situation, but it has possibilities.

—SAM GOLDWYN

Over the years, I've often been asked how I managed to keep up with all my different businesses. It puzzled many people. But one of the things they didn't see is how my businesses and activities fit together, so that I viewed it as managing one synergistic conglomerate rather than wrestling with an assortment of different ventures.

Some of my companies have shared office and warehouse space, computer services, a telephone system, and some personnel. By sharing this way, each business entity got better things than it could afford on its own, and no entity spent more than it had to for its needs. There was synergy. For example, one company produced videos and serviced a number of my consulting clients with infomercial and promotional video production. It also produced videos that my publishing company sold. My publishing company's catalogues also advertised my consulting, copywriting, and speaking services. My speaking activities provided new customers for my publishing company's mailing lists. The books I wrote for other publishers, which were sold in bookstores, provided new customers for my company's mailing lists and provided consulting clients, so I counted my writing as a form of advertising.

I carefully and strategically started, acquired, and developed businesses and business interests that were profitable and valuable in and of themselves, but that also assisted each other, so that the whole was greater than the parts. Many savvy entrepreneurs follow this same pattern.

On a bigger scale, consider the Disney empire. Its cable-TV Disney Channel is a business in and of itself but is also a huge promotional tool for its parks, movies, videos, and products. Its character-licensing business is immensely profitable, and everywhere those famous characters appear, they silently, subtly advertise other Disney products. Disney's mail-order business advertises its movies and parks and cross-promotes its retail stores. And on and on it goes.

Dan Kennedy's Eternal Truth #19

A normal small-business can only yield a normal small-business income. To earn an extraordinary income, you must develop an extraordinary business!

This kind of "cross-fertilization," done carefully and intelligently, on a big or small scale, can make your business more profitable and a lot more fun. This is the way to milk a big income out of a small business.

Strengthen Your Conglomerate with Strategic Alliances

A longtime friend and business associate started a travel agency. The guarantee of my business alone made this an attractive business venture for him. For my allegiance, I got the convenience of instant, direct, unlimited access to the computer, the diligence of his staff, discounts, and some perks. But our alliance went further.

His travel agency and my speaking/seminar business shared the cost and use of an employee with computer skills. We shared a computer system. This resulted in my getting many of my mailing lists ship-shape at a bargain cost. For my $3,495-per-person direct-marketing conferences, his agency handled all the calls, airline and hotel reservations, and travel arrangements for my attendees and speakers. This arrangement provided my clients with an enhanced service and freed up my own staff from time-consuming responsibilities. It provided his agency with customers—and commissions—he'd never have received otherwise, with no marketing costs.

I created another alliance many years ago when my fledgling company lacked a solid credit standing and was having difficulty getting open credit with major vendors. A business friend of mine and I struck a bargain: I provided free consulting for some of his direct-mail projects and free use of my in-house recording studio for his occasional audio projects. In return, his more established company guaranteed an open credit line with the vendors I needed to do business with.

These kinds of strategic alliances work to everyone's benefits. Some may be created to further sales, others to reduce costs. Either way, they can go a long way toward bolstering bottom line.

How to Get Rich by Accident

The way to wealth as an entrepreneur is continually, creatively redefining and reinventing a business. Entrepreneurs need to be open to and alert for completely unexpected opportunities for alliances and ways to expand businesses on top of the business. When you can do this, you can just about get rich by accident.

The large mail-order marketer of office supplies, Quill Corporation, provides a good example. They got in the mail-order business completely by accident. They originally had a tiny, struggling retail business; in an attempt to attract business, the owners experimented with sending out new product announcements and special offers on postcards. The response to their simple direct-mail campaigns was so good, they started selling directly rather than through the retail system.

The Miller Brothers started Quill in 1957 in a remodeled coal bin in Chicago with $2,000.00 they managed to scrape together. Today, they mail more than 45 million pieces a year, serve more than 850,000 customers, generate hundreds of millions of dollars in annual sales. "Being in the mail-order business was never our intention," Jack Miller says. "It just sort of happened."

I had a client in the industrial chemicals business who discovered his employees sneaking bottles of one of their products out the back door and selling it to friends and neighbors. To their eternal credit, instead of putting an armed guard at the back door, the firm instead seized opportunity, reasoning if it's good enough to steal and sell to consumers, we ought to be selling it to consumers. Today, the sales of that one product bottled for consumer use and sold on TV, in catalogs, and in retail chains—including Home Depot and Wal-Mart—far exceed the entire sales volume of the original business.

I also have an example from my own experience.

- *Puzzle piece #1.* In 1982, I was in my third year guest lecturing for a large-practice management firm in the chiropractic field. The firm charged its clients $30,000.00 each for a multi-year package of seminars and services. Just about every competitor in the field sold similarly expensive services, requiring big commitments.
- *Puzzle piece #2.* While speaking for this firm, I met another speaker with whom I was tremendously impressed. I

believed then and still believe he was the very best motivational speaker ever. But I discovered, incredibly, that he wasn't working much.

- *Puzzle piece #3.* At the time, one of my businesses was a custom audiocassette manufacturing, packaging, and publishing company specializing in producing materials for professional speakers. I was stuck with the small, tight margins of a manufacturer and was urgently in need of increased revenue.

Then I put the pieces together. I detected an "opportunity gap." I figured if we went to these doctors with an offer of practice-building guidance priced a lot less than what was currently available, we'd have a unique opportunity to scoop up the majority who wanted help but wouldn't or couldn't commit to a high investment. So we built an audiocassette-based product around the idea, using this fantastic speaker, to be produced and controlled by my manufacturing company. Then we created a new seminar company and used direct mail to put 30 to 40 doctors in each free seminar, four or five nights a week in four or five different cities, where we sold the cassette-based systems for $499.00 to $899.00.

From 1983 to 1985, this business venture sold millions of dollars worth of merchandise. It provided a lot of work and an excellent income to the speaker, and it provided a lot of work for my manufacturing plant at much better-than-average profit margins. It even built a presence in that niche market and a mailing list that continues to generate profits today, purely via mail order. This multimillion-dollar business was a happy accident.

Careful expansion and diversification, linking businesses within a business, forming strategic alliances, and keeping the doors wide open to accidental, additional opportunity all can give the small-business entrepreneur a big income—a huge fortune.

The Secret of Giving Them More of What They Want (and Less of What They Don't)

This is as good a time as any to sneak in a big secret, a big opportunity, and a big reason most business owners fail to realize even a small portion of their income potential.

Oddly, most business owners sell what they want to sell.

They do *not* determine exactly what their customers want, then offer that.

Let me tell you about the evolution of Jerry Jones' business. Jerry is a Platinum Member of mine who publishes a nifty little magazine called *Healthy, Wealthy, and Wise,* which he sells in quantity to dentists, who give subscriptions to all their patients. Each dentist gets his own promotional insert in the issues sent to his patients. Hundreds of thousands of copies are mailed each month. The documented result is substantially increased referrals for the dentists.

For quite a while, Jerry thought he was in the business of publishing this newsletter for dental patients as a service to dentists. Then he surveyed his customers to see if they would be interested in other hands-off, done-for-them marketing, and discovered a high interest in having postcard mailings done to new move-ins, to past patients, etc. This doubled yes, doubled—Jerry's business virtually overnight. And this redefined the business as a direct-marketing company serving the dental profession.

Since then, Jerry has added other do-it-for-them marketing—and most recently—time-efficient tele-coaching for dentists eager to be more aggressive, diversified, and sophisticated with their marketing. Again redefining the business as a full-service marketing company.

The point is that Jerry started taking the pulse of his clients, probing for unmet needs and desires, then creating new products and services to meet those specific needs and desires.

The Antidote to Advertising

Yes, I'm an "ad man," but I recognize that for most business owners, advertising remains an expensive and frustrating mystery. I'm a marketing guy, but I understand that most business owners prefer other aspects of business and are least comfortable with marketing. If this is you and you find the entire responsibility of advertising and marketing to obtain new customers painful and problematic, there is a simple solution: do a lot more business with the customers you do get—so you need less of them. That begs a "miniconglomerate" approach.

Rory Fatt of Restaurant Marketing Systems teaches this to restaurant owners. He shows them how to be in the birthday party/celebration business, catering business, prepared frozen gourmet meals business. Another of my Members, Michael Attias, also works with restaurant owners showing them how to niche-market to pharmaceutical sales reps to cater and deliver in-office luncheons to the doctors' offices they call on. Lester Nathan, profit improvement consultant to pharmacies, shows them how to add proprietary, private-label pain relief products to better market their compounding services. Their focus is the same: reduce the need for new and more customers by offering more diverse products and services to fewer customers.

CHAPTER 16

Using Your Business as a Path to Financial Independence

The only thing worse than not getting what you want is getting what you want.

—OSCAR WILDE

Why are you in business or getting into business?

You might be surprised at some of the answers I get when I ask this question of clients or at seminars. You see, getting into business is actually pretty easy, even too easy for some people's own good. Getting in is often a lot easier than getting out. And getting in is definitely a lot easier than getting what you really want from being in business. That's the tough assignment.

For starters, viewing your business as "the end" is a mistake. It's not an achieved goal; it is a means for achieving many other goals. For too many people, the desire to own their own business is so powerful and exciting that little thought is given to "what's next?"

You don't want to marry the business. Marry the goals.

Years ago, in connection with a writing assignment, I interviewed a woman in the muffin business in Atlanta. Her name has long since been forgotten, so I'll call her Margie.

Margie's experience provides a great example. Margie determined that she wanted to open her own muffin and cookie store. She researched the field, found a location she believed was viable, and developed some of her own creative recipes. She was very excited about her business plan. At night, she lay awake, staring at the ceiling, visualizing her sign—Margie's Famous Muffins and Munchies—over the door of her store.

After some struggle to get the money together, Margie opened her shop just as she had visualized it. Just one month later, she was in financial trouble. The location wasn't as "hot" as she'd believed, and there were other problems. But, by happy accident, the manager of a nearby supermarket chain stopped in and was so impressed with Margie's muffins that he asked her to supply products for resale in his stores. That was a big success, quickly requiring a full night-shift operation to meet the demand.

The retail store was losing money, but the wholesale baking operation was a success. Finally, Margie did the obvious and closed down the high-rent, unsuccessful retail location and put the wholesale baking operation in a cheap rental space. But she cried for a week over the death of her dream. By the end of that year, she was supplying more supermarkets plus numerous restaurants and making a huge net profit. By not having to be at her retail business every day, she had the opportunity to expand by selling new accounts. She had the makings of an enormously successful business. But it was not the business she originally mentally married, and that caused her quite a bit of emotional distress. Her emotional difficulties came from being too focused on "modus operandi" rather than life goals.

Don't Let Your Business Own You

It's ironic that in order to get what you really want from owning your own business—wealth, security, freedom, for example— you must do the most unnatural, difficult thing for an entrepreneur: you must systematically reduce the dependency of the business on you. Don't overlook this. This is *the* secret to becoming financially independent through entrepreneurship.

Most entrepreneurs have no understanding of this and give it very little thought until it's too late. They wind up being owned by their businesses. To their surprise, they find that

There's an old joke about the government bureaucrat descending on the small-business owner. He says, "We've received a report that you have some poor fellow working here 18 hours a day, seven days a week, for nothing but a room, board, meals, all the tobacco he can smoke, and all the liquor he can drink. Is that true?" "Yes, I'm afraid it is," admits the owner. "And I'm sad to say, you're looking at him."

they've traded one old boss for a plethora of new ones: stock-holders, investors and lenders, employees and associates, customers and clients, vendors, and government agencies.

You're probably wondering about the security of your business. If the typical entrepreneur leaves the business alone for a week, it does a Jekyll-Hyde transformation. You have got to be there! I know many business owners who go years without a vacation. And those who do go on vacation, don't enjoy it. He half hopes everything's OK back at the ranch, which he checks every few hours by phone, but he's half disappointed if it is OK. After all, how could it be without his indispensable presence?

Too many people get into business only to discover they've acquired a new, tougher, more demanding, more stressful job, and they cannot see any way to change it.

The trick is to let the business mature—and the faster, the better. Immature business is entrepreneur-driven. In its early days, that's OK and usually necessary. You are the business. From day one, though, if your business is to provide security, freedom, and wealth, you should be working at weaning the business from dependence on *you* and creating dependence on *systems*. My friend Ken Varga, who has built huge companies, says any business still dependent on your day-to-day presence after three years is not a business at all. It's a job.

I've appeared as a speaker on several programs with Michael Gerber, author of the best-selling book *The E-Myth*. His advice is to systemize your business as if you would franchise it and replicate it in a hundred distant sites, even if you have no intention of doing so. Good, liberating strategy. My client Chet Rowland owns the largest pest control company in central Florida, growing each year by double-digit percentages, yet he spends fewer than five hours a week at its offices, possibly because of his incredibly thorough, microscopically detailed systems and checklists for every function.

Getting Out of Your Own Way

Some people tie their egos up in their minute-by-minute, indispensable importance to their businesses. I have made this mistake myself: carrying data around in my head, making every decision myself whether for a dime or a dollar, being the first one at office in the morning, the last one there at the end of the day. I was the guy with the beeper and a cellular phone, able to do every job in the place—and meddling in every one of them.

I was probably indispensable and irreplaceable. I was also stressed out—a nervous breakdown looking for a place to happen. I started getting in the habit of stopping off "for a couple of drinks" after leaving the office and going home hours later half-drunk. This is not the way to get your sense of importance satisfied.

Instead, you can be important and make the most meaningful contributions to your business—without sacrificing your health, family, and sanity—by freeing yourself from in-depth involvement in day-to-day operations, so you have more time for the few business-building things you do best. In my case, in my publishing company, what I did best was create new products or improve the ones we already had, create advertising and marketing materials, and deal with key clients and contacts. If I gave equal time to purchasing raw materials and supplies, bookkeeping, organizing records and mailing lists, product quality control, and so on, I cheated the business out of my best; and I cheated myself out of the business's best.

Be sure you're not cheating yourself and your business out of your best.

How to Help Your Business Mature

A mature business is some or all of the following things:

- MARKET driven
- PRODUCT driven
- SERVICE driven
- SYSTEMS driven

For example, a retail store in a busy mall is driven by its *market*. Very little, if any, outside advertising or marketing is done; the business is designed to feed off the mall traffic. A manufacturer of a little widget that goes inside a bigger widget that makes the windshield wiper switch work is driven by its product. The bigger widget maker has to have the little widget; the little widget is only made by a couple of companies. A quick-copy shop is driven by its service; its customers are usually concerned with and wooed by speed, convenience, and reliability.

In the beginning, these businesses will also be *owner driven*. The retail-store owner makes all the product, pricing, window-display, and other decisions for the store. The manufacturer watches over the widget making, hiring, firing, buying raw materials, keeping the customers happy, and so on. The copy-shop owner solicits accounts, deals with customers, and keeps the copy shop hopping.

Over time, these businesses can mature to a great degree. The owners can isolate the one or two things they do best and delegate the rest. But the way to get to that stage is to develop systems, and the development of effective *marketing systems* is the most vital job overlooked by most entrepreneurs.

For example, consider John G., a roofing contractor. He told me that he wanted to diminish his day-to-day work in the business, but because he is the one who brings in most of the business, he doesn't know how to go about it. He's been able to hire good crews and good managers and delegate all the labor, but, he asked, how do you delegate the prospecting and selling that gets the jobs?

The answer is to develop a marketing system that delivers predictable results from repetitive use. In John's case, we worked together to create a direct-mail campaign aimed at qualified leads (provided by a list broker), then a telephone procedure to convert a predictable number of those inquiries to appointments. Then, the big step, we worked on a standardized sales presentation using a flip chart, a video, and a cost-quoting computer program. This made it possible to hire sales representatives, train them quickly and easily, and put them in the field to secure just about the same number of jobs per appointments as when John dealt personally with all the customers. Bingo! This fellow was able to replace himself with a marketing system.

Dan Kennedy's
Eternal Truth #20

Passion wanes with longevity
and familiarity.

Over the next two years, not only did John achieve his objective of cutting by half his time devoted to the business, but the business was able to increase by nearly 30%!

The time to start thinking about all this is not 6 or 12 months before you'd like to change your role in your business. In fact, you should start planning for flexibility and change from day one. You must accept that the unbridled passions you feel for your business at the beginning, that has you happily there from dawn to midnight up to your armpits in work, will change as time passes. The activity you can't wait to get at today may bore the blazes out of you three years from now. It's smart to build your business in a way that allows you to satisfy your changing interests.

You can also think of this as a form of insurance. You could be injured or become ill. The statistics I've seen indicate that one of every three business owners experience some period of disability during their careers. For many, even with an insurance policy in their desk drawer, this can kill the business. Imagine, though, how much more likely it will be that your business can survive a period of months without you if you've structured it with systems from the very beginning.

The first thing you must do is ensure that the routine processes of your business are really routine. That means they happen by procedure so that just about anybody can step in and follow those procedures. You shouldn't have to have your nose in everything.

Second, you need to develop your business to the point where new customers or clients are attracted to your company by marketing systems, not through your direct personal efforts.

Third, you must have a plan for directing more and more of your time and energy to the few aspects of the business you enjoy and do best and for reducing the commitment of your time and energy to the many aspects of the business you do not enjoy or do best.

How Does a System Work?

First and foremost, a system works without you being married to it 24 hours a day. Let's say there have been a number of burglaries in your neighborhood, and you are suddenly more concerned than usual with making your home look occupied all the time. One way to do that is to stay home. Another would be to hire a house-sitter for the times you aren't there—in other words, delegating the responsibility. Or, you could get some simple, inexpensive electronic devices that can be set to turn different lights and appliances on and off at different times. That would be a system. Once in place, it works with little or no attention from you.

Systems deliver predictable and consistent results.

A marketing system is arguably the most important kind of system that an entrepreneur can ever give the business. One restaurant owner I know, Bill H., exemplifies the success of initiating such a system. He sends two letters and a postcard to residents of the neighborhoods surrounding his restaurant and to people in businesses around his restaurant. He has this system streamlined to the point that he has a formula for determining what percentage of response he will get from each mailing and how many of those responses turned into reservations and revenue for his restaurant. This means he can guarantee his restaurant a certain predictable base of business each and every week. If, say, a seasonal slump is coming up, he can increase the number of letters mailed in order to increase revenue. He can go to sleep at night knowing that a certain number of new clients will call the next day, and, because this is an entirely mechanical process, he could go on vacation for three weeks and still guarantee a certain amount of business to his restaurant. His system gives him immense power, leverage of time, less stress and frustration, and better positioning with new clients.

Always strive to put systems in place; the right systems can totally transform a business.

CHAPTER 17

How to Get a
Business Out of Trouble

*One ought never to turn one's back on a threatened danger and try
to run away from it. If you do that, you will double the danger.
But if you meet it promptly and without flinching, you will
reduce it by half. Never run away from anything. Never.*

—WINSTON CHURCHILL

opefully you'll never need the advice in this brief chapter.
Hopefully.

I have been involved in a couple of business turn-
arounds and helped clients with others. I've also made a point of
studying some of the best-known, big-name turnaround experts,
and I can tell you that there is very little difference between getting one business or another out of trouble. Your options for
action are rather limited.

The very first, crucial step is honesty. You've got to forget all
about protecting your ego and blaming others. None of that matters when the kettle is boiling over. You have to diagnose and
identify problems, period. You need all the gory details. No one

can be allowed to hide anything; no one can be allowed to feel they have to hide anything.

This is very tough to achieve. Everybody's natural responses are to cover their own tracks as best they can. If people can't or won't be honest with themselves and each other about the problems, either the people have to go, fast, or the business goes under. That's it.

As Long as There's a Pulse, There's Hope

The only absolutely certain death blow for a troubled business is running out of cash. There's little else that's irreversible.

Poisoned Tylenol killed people, but the business survived. Automakers routinely recall thousands of cars with potentially lethal defects, but most survive. Key people quit, big competitors move in, fires and floods happen, but businesses survive. I don't think there's any business problem that can't be beat as long as there's cash flow. During a turnaround period, profit and loss is even irrelevant. But cash flow is everything.

Forget "Kinder" and "Gentler"

Cut costs with the ax, not a surgical knife. If there's any turnaround mistake I've made more than once, it's being too gentle and conservative in the cutting. You can always put a person or function back in if you must. To start getting out of trouble, though, swing your ax in a wide arc. Cut everywhere. Spare no one, no thing. Cut, cut, cut.

In one turnaround situation, I let 38 people go in one day. I had more blood on my hands than the monster in a cheap horror movie. It was really awful. One of the top people asked me,

I've run a company completely out of cash on two occasions. Miraculously, the company got through both these situations. On one of those occasions, the company took five weeks to recover from a $47,000.00 checking account overdraft. I spent those five weeks walking around with just a few crinkled dollar bills in my pocket, coasting downhill in my car to conserve gas, jumping out of my skin at every phone call, just waiting for the final death nudge to come from somewhere. I've faced cash-flow problems since, but I learned my lesson. No matter the pressure, I will not take a business down to zero cash.

If you find your business in a cash-flow crunch, you must immediately become very tight-fisted about parting with each penny. Pay bills in tiny pieces. Trickle it out. Negotiate new terms with vendors as fast as you can. Sacrifice some vendors if you must. Put tiny dabs of grease on the squeakiest wheels. But never, never spend down to zero or, worse, below zero to appease the wolves. Let them stand out there baying and scratching at the door, but keep a few spare bullets in your gun at all times.

"How do you know you can function without some of these people?" I said, "I don't." I really didn't. I didn't have time to sort out who was really important and who wasn't. I had to stop the cash hemorrhage first, to even get a minute to think. So I swung the ax with abandon. And I'd do it again without a second thought if presented with a similar situation.

Pull Together a Plan

Once you've done what you can to stop the cash from pouring out of the business' wounds, bring everything to a near stop for a few days, get the best brains together you can, lock yourselves up in a quiet room without interruptions, and pull together a plan.

Without a plan, you'll make the mistake I made in the first turnaround crisis I dealt with. I started out by instantly reacting to each and every new problem that reared its ugly head, each howling wolf as it appeared at the door. I'd drop one thing to face the other, then turn from that to the next noise in the dark. Pretty soon I was spinning around like a top. One night, long after

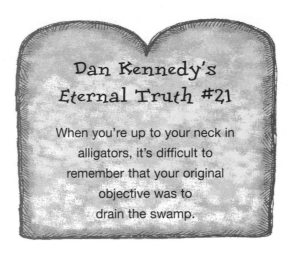

Dan Kennedy's
Eternal Truth #21

When you're up to your neck in alligators, it's difficult to remember that your original objective was to drain the swamp.

everybody else had left, I was in my chair behind my desk, sweaty, bone tired, exhausted. I realized I was completely out of control.

Then I shut the door and put together a believable, step-by-step business plan with a lot of details for the first six months and more general ideas for the next six. With this battle plan in hand, I had confidence, I had the ability to engineer cooperation from others. Then I placed a limit on the amount of time each day dedicated to problems. When we hit the quota for the day, that was it; the rest of the problems had to stand in line until the next day. Each day, I set aside a certain amount of time to implement the business plan. With plan in hand, I restored order and kept myself out of the padded room.

Don't Hide

If your business owes a lot of money to a lot of creditors, you'll be tempted to hide. Big mistake. You or someone you give this responsibility to must keep the lines of communication open for those creditors and be as truthful as possible with them. When you can't promise a payment amount and date, don't; promise what you can, even if that's only the date and time you'll next communicate.

Target the creditors hurting your cash flow most for comprehensive renegotiation. Take your new business plan and meet in person if possible. At the least, phone or fax them, and shoot for the very best deal you can get.

For example, let's say you owe XYZ Company $20,000.00, all past due. You might get that $20,000.00 switched from a trade payable to a long-term, five-year installment note, interest only for the first year, and agree on new purchases to pay one-third with order, one-third on delivery, and one-third in 30 days. This takes $20,000.00 out of your current struggle altogether. Otherwise, you'd be whacking away at that $500.00 or $1,000.00 at a time, the creditor would never be happy, and getting needed goods would probably be next to impossible.

Facing trouble head-on, more often than not, earns respect and promotes cooperation.

Don't Take It Personally

OK, your business is in trouble, and you were captain of the ship while it smashed into the rocks. That's bad. But everybody makes mistakes. You're not the first, you won't be the last, and there is no shame in screwing up. The only cause for shame would be giving up without a fight. If you are genuinely trying to do the best you can, there's nothing to be ashamed of.

Beating yourself up or letting somebody else beat you up as a person is uncalled for and, obviously, unproductive. You have to be able to step out of the emotion and be a tough-minded turn-around consultant for your own business.

Direct Your Energy to Business Renovation

Even if it's only an hour, grab a certain amount of time each and every day and go to work on reinventing your business. Get to the very core of the problems. During a turnaround, you'll be doing a lot of patching work, and that's OK, but while you're patching up cuts and bruises, you need to be the visionary designer of a whole new and improved operation.

Don G. had a chain of six restaurants that wound up in deep trouble. While he did all the things we've been talking about with the entire chain, he also took just one of the locations as his "new" model and made major changes there, literally inventing a new and different restaurant operation, from A to Z. After a year, the entire company had limped its way back into positive cash flow, largely through debt restructuring and cost-cutting, and although the entire business was still operating at a net loss, the new model was consistently hitting a 30% profit mark. Don now had a model to duplicate in his other five locations, which allowed him to again restructure debt, get some new investment capital, and quickly make over the other five locations. By the end of the second year of the turnaround, he had chalked up several hundred thousand dollars in profit.

At this point, the local beer distributor who supplied his restaurants bought into his company and contributed enough capital to wipe out all the high-interest debt and open four more locations. Three years later, they sold the entire business to a national food-service company and walked away millionaires.

If Don had waited until he had his entire turnaround process implemented to go to work on his core business's reinvention, all these good things would not have happened, and he might have run out of time and money before ever getting to try his new plan.

CHAPTER 18

A No B.S. Report on
the Internet and Other
Technology

*You know you've lost control of your computer when the mouse
orders from the International House of Cheese's Web site
on the Internet.*

—Dr. Herb True

Since the first version of this book was published in 1993,
the world has seen a huge explosion in the types and quality of technology available.

The dotcom boom has come and crashed, but most entrepreneurs are still seduced and entranced by the Internet. In my view,
making money via the Internet is grossly overhyped. Let's examine some of the claims.

- Millions and millions of people are flooding onto the Net,
  running around looking at Web sites, and buying everything that isn't nailed down.
- If you don't have your own Web site and e-mail address,
  you're as much out of touch as somebody still writing letters

with a manual typewriter or washing clothes on a rock in the river.

- The gold rush is now. The longer you wait, the more expensive and difficult it will be to get involved.
- Using the Internet is like getting free advertising—how can you say no to that?

Now I'd like to give you my no B.S. take on these claims, and I want to qualify it a bit. First, I'll confess I'm far from a "techie." I use my computer as a typewriter, and I don't like it very much. So there's no doubt I come to discussions of technology with a bias. I'm known as a Luddite. However, I should also mention that I am the marketing advisor to several of the most highly respected experts in the Internet field. Two of my Platinum Inner Circle Members are highly respected Internet-marketing gurus, software developers, and industry leaders: Corey Rudl and Yanik Silver. Another, Matt Furey, does well over $150,000.00 a month in sales at his Web sites. And my own businesses utilize Internet marketing.

With skepticism high but hope intact, I continually look at everything all my clients, subscribers, and researchers can find, produce, or suggest with regard to making money via the Internet.

With all that said, here are some of the hard, cold realities about this fascinating, promising, but still largely disappointing media. The time has come when it must be used and can be used profitably, but realistic, reasonable expectations are vital.

Knock, Knock, Who's There?

Let's start with the millions of people who are online, using the Internet. The truth is that nobody, and I mean nobody, knows the real number of users. When you see companies like America Online and CompuServe talk about the huge number of new subscribers to their services each month, you need to know the number of dropouts, too. As near as I can tell, in any given time period, they lose about as many as they gain. If you subtract from the number of primary users those under the age of 16, the number of students, government agencies, and others using it only for research, and the vast majority of business people using it only for e-mail, who do you have left? And keep in mind you'll be competing for attention with tens of thousands of other Web sites in a disorganized, chaotic environment.

What Are Internet Users Really Buying?

One of the many obstacles to making money on the Internet is that those things that cyberspace browsers are really interested in may not match up with what you have to sell. Although it is difficult to get any reliable numbers, a compilation of experts' educated guesses indicates that 30% to 60% of all commerce on the Internet has to do with one thing and one thing only—sex.

Even the staid *Wall Street Journal* has run a front page article on the millions of dollars being made with sex-related goods and services on the Internet. Its article featured a former strip club dancer named Danni Ashe detailing her success on the Internet selling adult videos, magazines, autographed pictures, used underwear, and access to chat rooms and interactive activities. And she is not alone. Many other publications have even more exhaustedly covered this same subject. Virtually everybody who was and is selling sex-related entertainment via magazines and 900 telephone numbers has rushed to the Internet. Their extraordinary prosperity tells you a lot about the average cyberspace customer and just what that customer is interested in buying.

It is easy to get a sense of the types of sites people are most responsive to by checking traffic counts through the major search engines such as Yahoo and Google. You'll find "sex" gets the highest visitor counts, by giant margins.

To be fair, "health" is another very heavily trafficked category. And to be fair, there are many categories where successful Web-based businesses exist.

To spotlight opportunity, there's no doubt e-commerce is real, for everything from hard-to-find wines to mortgages to, of course, the poster child, Amazon.com. To reveal a "secret," the vast majority of my clients profiting from the Internet use offline advertising to drive online traffic *and* use offline marketing to sell to online-created leads. This is especially important for local businesses doing business only in their own area.

Be There or Be Square

Now let's tackle the second idea that if you don't have your own Web sites and e-mail address on your business card and aren't actively marketing with the Internet, everybody will think you're some kind of dinosaur, hopelessly out of touch. Unless you are in a technology oriented business, this simply isn't true.

It's not that clear-cut. You should use Web sites, e-mail marketing, and possibly purchased search engine traffic, but you certainly shouldn't let yourself be stampeded into it. The Internet is full of Web sites put up by business people pressured into doing so that are badly designed, unproductive, and now neglected. Huge sums of money are wasted by people feeling forced or hurried to get on the Internet just because their competitors are there or because they've heard so much about it. My favorite western philosopher, Texas Bix Bender, author of the book *Don't Squat with Yer Spurs On*, observed that "just 'cause you're following a well-marked trail don't mean that whoever made it knew where they were goin'."

It's very unlikely to get more expensive to get involved with the Internet in the future. In fact, the opposite is going to be true, just as it has been with all technology. Today's fax machines cost one-fifth as much as the early models did. I remember paying $299.00 for my first hand-held calculator. Today, you can buy a better one for $9.95. In the beginning, it was common to pay thousands to tens of thousands of dollars to have a Web site designed; now the cost is under $5,000.00 in most cases, and there's even off-the-shelf software that lets you do it yourself.

My point is, proceed cautiously, based on strategy, not panic or peer pressure.

But the Gold Rush Is On and You Don't Want to Be Last, Do You?

How about the gold rush idea? The promoters of Web sites and Internet malls love using the analogy that this is like the great gold rush and those who get there first will get the gold. Another analogy they love is the real estate comparison: get a prime spot in this mall now, before the price skyrockets. These analogies are ridiculous because unlike gold mines and locations in physical malls, there is an unlimited amount of Internet space. People can make as many Web sites as they want, and an Internet mall doesn't actually have any prime sites. Will Rogers advised, "Buy real estate because they ain't making more of it." Well, they ARE making more real estate on the Internet—lots of it.

The people who sold the shovels to the gold miners made more money than most miners did. So far, that is definitely true of the Internet. The people selling Web sites, mall sites, and services are making a lot more money than the Internet merchants buying them. Be especially suspicious of those promoting Internet opportunities and services who make money with the Internet only as shovel sellers.

Is There a Free Lunch on the Internet?

If there is a universal, eternal no B.S. truth about life, it is that "there ain't no free lunch." Ever. But that sure doesn't stop us from looking for it, does it? To quote Texas Bix Bender again: "You can always find free cheese in a mousetrap." Yep.

That brings us to the free advertising claim of the Internet. Your Web site might be seen by tens of thousands or even millions of people at almost no cost to you. Or you can use e-mail to send out thousands of sales messages with no printing or postage costs. Free marketing!

This is obviously attractive. But the odds of people just stumbling across your Web site and becoming your customers are about the same as the odds of winning the lottery or being struck twice by lightning. You have to do things to bring prospective customers to your Web site, and all of those things either cost money or are incredibly labor-intensive, which means they cost time and, therefore, money.

If you decide to use the free direct mail offered by e-mail, you'd better watch out. Since its birth as a research tool, the

Internet has been an adamantly anti-commercial environment. The proliferation of e-mail has led to anti-spam laws in place and pending at state and federal levels, Internet servers routinely cutting off people they suspect of sending large numbers of unsolicited e-mail, and most people having one or more spam-blocking devices on their own sites. Using e-mail for marketing purposes is still possible, but very tricky, generally requiring much greater expertise than the novice or casual Internet user possesses. And it is NOT free. It requires either time or money spent on outside services.

In Spite of All That, Should You Be Devoting Serious Attention to Marketing Your Business via the Internet?

To be fair, let me quickly give you some good news: Internet users and shoppers tend, demographically, to be high income, above-average in education, relatively sophisticated people with diverse interests. For many businesses, these are very desirable customers.

If you're interested in global commerce, the Internet attracts a lot of people from every imaginable country. Through my Web site, we've acquired customers in Greece, Russia, Germany, France, England, Australia, New Zealand, Japan, Korea, and Taiwan.

Internet browsers tend to spend a lot of time at Web sites that interest them. For example, the Sharper Image catalog people report that the average time spent at their Web site by a browser is more than 10 minutes. Warner Brothers Studio Stores reports an average of 32 minutes. Visitors to my sites are spending 10 to 30 minutes. Facts like these are encouraging and stimulating to anybody with a marketing-oriented mind.

Companies everywhere are spending a whole lot of money trying to figure out how they can turn the Internet into a truly viable marketplace and marketing medium. We are making progress constantly.

The Future May Be Permission-Only Marketing On and Off the Internet

In 2003, anti-spam activity was at an all-time high, but the Internet was not the only battleground. The Do Not Call List chilled telemarketing, and—incredibly—even prompted Senator Schumer of New York to speculate about a Do Not Mail List. A much stronger law restricting use of broadcast fax nearly went into effect, delayed into 2004 via last-minute reprieve. Everywhere you look, unwanted marketing is under attack. For 20 years, I've been using a story in my speeches too lengthy to recount here, to demonstrate the importance of positioning yourself as a Welcome Guest rather than Annoying Pest. Seems the world has caught up to my advice.

As I write this book, there may be no single more important task than to "lock in" your absolute right to communicate as you wish with your own past and present customers or clients, as even this process is challenged by new and pending laws, some with very stiff penalties. I've been helping all my clients add language to their order forms, contracts, client profiles, etc. that includes something like this:

> *Providing the above contact information including your address, phone number, FAX number and e-mail address constitutes permission for us to communicate with you via these means.*

My clients are not alone in this. Just today, I got a fax from Airborne Express asking me to update my customer information, and the form contained comparable language.

We have acknowledged the wisdom of having signed permission-to-communicate documents on file. You should too.

Arguably of equal importance, you should increase your efforts to nurture good relationships with customers so that they do welcome you when you arrive—via whatever media.

Similar language is rapidly getting added to online and offline forms, coupons, etc. obtained from prospects requesting information from a company.

As we head into a time when the individual is barraged by and resistant to a rising flood of communication through an ever-increasing number of channels, the astute entrepreneur will think more and more in terms of "permission" and "relationship." I teach, incidentally, that businesses need to move away from transactional operation to relationship-based operation.

The Fax as a Marketing Machine

As reluctant as I have been to express much enthusiasm for the Internet, I have been in love with the fax machine. It's my opinion that the fax machine is the greatest marketing invention made during my lifetime. Let me explain why I feel that way.

It's a marketing truth that it is easier and more profitable to sell more to existing customers than to get new customers, and fax communication is an excellent way to communicate with customers, frequently at a dirt-cheap cost. Customers are usually willing to provide their fax numbers and eager to get timely information from you via fax. It has the impact of immediacy, like FedEx, even more so than e-mail. It provides greater format and cosmetic-look flexibility than e-mail.

Taking inbound orders by fax is very exciting. It provides the impulse-buy opportunity without (or in addition to) a manned 800-number. In businesses like mine, an order received by fax is much better than the same order called in over the phone for several reasons, including the cost of taking the order and accuracy of the information.

Even very small businesses can benefit. For example, it's an increasing trend in restaurants for take-out orders to come in by fax and be ready at a separate pick-up window.

When prospecting for new business by direct mail, including a simple form that prospective customers can fax back to request more information almost always boosts responses. The ease and immediacy of faxing back a form beats the delayed reaction time involved in mailing it and is less threatening to a timid prospect than calling.

Broadcast fax to "cold" prospects, to rented lists—the fax equivalent of spam—still exists, and often works, as of this writing, but it is increasingly legally problematic. In Canada, however, it is wide-open legal, and many of my clients who've stopped using it within the United States continue using it to market to Canada.

By the way, if you want to communicate with me, you can fax me at: (602) 269-3113. I like to hear from customers and clients and encourage orders to be placed by fax. This allows us to run a collection of businesses very efficiently with the absolute minimum of staff.

I love the fax machine.

Voice Mail as a Marketing Tool: The Magic of the Free Recorded Message

In and of itself, the free recorded message is not a panacea and should be used in concert with other smart techniques. But it is clear that offering additional information or free literature to prospective customers via a free recorded message—compared with requiring prospects to call a regular business number and talk with a live salesperson—almost always boosts responses. At the same time, the recorded message lets you, the marketer, run ads, send out mailings, and handle all the initial response without any significant staff requirements, and without your having to take calls personally.

Today, voice-mail options for marketing purposes range from the simple to the incredibly sophisticated and complex. Voice mail can be linked to regular or toll-free numbers, of any length, recorded using your voice or other voice(s) of your choice, with or without background music. It can capture leads by asking a caller to record name, address, etc.; letting a caller choose options from a menu to hear the choice of messages; giving a caller the option of being transferred from the recording to a real person; or it can be linked to fax-on-demand.

There's even a Find Me option. Let's say you run a carpet cleaning business. A person calls to hear your free recorded message about "Ten things you need to know before hiring any carpet cleaner." At the end, your customer can leave his or her name and address to have your brochure and coupons sent by mail. But what if the customer is impressed, ready to hire you, and wants to talk to somebody immediately? No problem. You give the customer that choice, he hits the star key on his phone, and— zap—your customer is transferred to your regular office phone. But what if you're a one-person operator? No problem. When your customer hits that button, he is transferred to your cell phone. If you don't answer after four rings, he is transferred to your home phone, then your office phone. At the same time, this system can notify you of the call via your beeper.

In other words, you can figure out a number of response handling options that are right for your business and tie them into your voice mail.

There's also Voice Broadcast, the delivery of a produced voice message to 10, 100, 1,000 or 100,000 phones all at once, at nominal cost. Bill Glazer, my Platinum Member, marketing advisor to retailers, and publisher of my *No B.S. Marketing Letter*, has used voice broadcasts extensively and very successfully for his own menswear stores. Some messages are done in his voice, some in celebrity-impersonator voices, mimicking former President Clinton, Elvis, and Bugs Bunny. Another client of mine putting some 30,000 people a year through financial seminars replaced live humans with voice broadcast to confirm reservations, slashing more than $50,000.00 in costs and actually increasing the show-up rate.

A Complex Matrix of Communication and Marketing Technologies

Different combinations of these media are best for different businesses. The expert I work with most closely in this field is Ron Romano at Automated Marketing Solutions, and you can contact the firm for more information at 800-858-8889 or at www.findme leads.com.

The Amazing Power of Audio and Video Brochures

Admittedly, this is not new technology. But the costs keep coming down, and the value keeps going up.

I have developed talking brochures and talking sales letters for many different kinds of businesses and products, including multi-level network marketing, financial services and insurance, chiropractic care, business opportunities, and industrial equipment.

I like the talking brochure because it discourages skimming and lets you deliver a complete sales message, can offer multiple voices, sound effects, and music to make it more interesting, can include your customers' testimonials in their own voices, and can hold the attention of the listener longer than you'd be able to with printed material. I have seen the addition of this type of cassette to a direct-mail package double the number of responses.

Video brochures, often done in infomercial formats, can be extremely effective, especially in instances where product demonstrations can be made. Recently, we produced a powerful infomercial-type video brochure for my client, Paul Johnston, who owns Shed Shop Inc., a California builder of upscale backyard sheds.

Final Thoughts on Technology

There can be no "final" thoughts. In fact, things written in this chapter may be obsolete before the manuscript becomes a book on a shelf and finds its way to your desk. But I have a few universal thoughts that border on timeless principle, thoughts that might have been good advice when Bell was hollering at Watson one room away and will still be good advice when you are teleporting yourself across continents a la *Star Trek*.

First, I am just as opposed to technology for technology's sake as I am to creativity for creativity's sake. These things have to be held to the strict standards of practicality and profit.

It's very easy to be seduced by the hot, new technology that everybody is talking about, but it's important to keep things in perspective. Incorporate new technology into your entrepreneurial life and your business cautiously, always bearing in mind that it must measurably earn its keep. Hold it to the tough standard of profitability.

Second, just because a technology is "great" does not mean it is great for you or a priority for you to utilize. On the other hand, you must be careful not to ignore, neglect, or resist a technology because of your own personal preferences or resistance to having to learn yet another new "thing." The challenge is to make these decisions rationally, not emotionally; consciously, not unconsciously.

Third, avoid being overly dependent on any one media or technology. The worst number in business is one, period. Diversity is the key to stability and longevity.

Afterword

T hank you for the opportunity of sharing my viewpoints on entrepreneurship with you.

What does the quintessential entrepreneur want most?

Wealth? Power? Prominence? No, in truth, the entrepreneur longs for the same overwhelming human reward everyone else does: understanding and appreciation. I understand you, and I appreciate you. I hope that's come through in this book and that you will want to move forward from just reading my book to having some sort of continuing relationship.

Be sure to check the back of this book where you will find two special offers from me to you. I hope you will take advantage of both.

A Look at the Author's
Business Activities

Dan Kennedy is an entrepreneur who has started, bought, built, and sold a number of businesses, and developed a large, loyal, international following as an author, speaker, consultant, and coach.

His business adventures have included owning an advertising agency; interests in a cosmetic company with retail locations and independent distributors; an award and trophy company conducting business via mail-order and selling in volume to the U.S. Army, Navy, Air Force, and Marines, Boy Scouts of America, and more than 200 of the *Fortune* 500 companies; and a seminar company training more than 20,000 dentists and chiropractors. He once bought a publicly held custom manufacturing company "no money down," took it through a nearly successful turnaround and Chapter 11 reorganization, and ultimately sold its manufacturing operations to a competitor while retaining its publishing assets for a new business.

His own publishing business grew to feature more than 100 books, audiocassette courses, business tool kits, etc., with well over 40,000 active customers before it was sold in 1999 to Group M Publishing in Austin, Texas, which operates it under the brand name Kimble & Kennedy Publishing. Its entire catalog is online at www.dankennedyproducts.com.

His other publishing business based around his *No B.S. Marketing Letter* was sold in 2003 and now operates as Glazer-Kennedy Inner Circle LLC, providing information and benefits memberships to thousands of business owners and publishing the newsletter, which is the most widely subscribed-to newsletter about direct marketing, marketing, and entrepreneurial strategies. It also provides coaching to entrepreneurs via a tele-coaching program.

His Kennedy Inner Circle Inc. business manages three peer advisory/mastermind groups of diverse business owners that meet periodically and his Platinum Inner Circle, a peer advisory/mastermind group comprised exclusively of top marketing consultants to specific industries. Members pay from $5,000.00 to $12,000.00 each per year to participate.

Information about the newsletter, tele-coaching, and coaching groups is available at www.dankennedy.com.

Speaking

Dan has been a professional speaker for more than 25 years. For nine consecutive years, he appeared on THE #1 seminar tour in America, full-day, multispeaker "success rallies" in 25 to 28 locations a year, typically addressing audiences of 10,000 to 30,000. In these rallies, he shared the platform with numerous celebrities stories from all walks of life, including former U.S. Presidents Reagan, Ford, and Bush; General Colin Powell; General Norman

Schwartzkopf; such world leaders as Margaret Thatcher and Mikhail Gorbachov; attorneys Gerry Spence and Alan Dershowitz; Olympians Mary Lou Retton and Bonnie Blair; NFL Super Bowl quarterbacks Troy Aikman and Joe Montana; boxer George Foreman; broadcasters Paul Harvey and Larry King; legendary entrepreneurs Debbi Fields (Mrs. Fields Cookies), Jim McCann (1-800-Flowers), Ben & Jerry (Ben & Jerry's Ice Cream), and Mark McCormack (IMG, the giant sports management company); as well as some of America's most popular motivational speakers and sales trainers, including Zig Ziglar, Brian Tracy, Jim Rohn, and Tom Hopkins. Dan has spoken repeatedly to leading corporations such as Sun Securities, American Honda, and Pitney-Bowes and has frequently been a featured speaker at industry-specific multiday marketing boot camps requiring $2,000.00 to $7,000.00 per person to attend. These events include programs for dentists, chiropractors, lawyers, tax accountants, financial planners, carpet cleaners, photography studio owners, martial arts school owners, and on and on. For many of his more than 25 years in speaking, he delivered 60 to 70 presentations per year.

Consulting

As a consultant, Dan has applied his strategies in—at last count—156 different businesses, industries, professions, and product categories, with clients ranging from mom-and-pop merchants to *Fortune* 500 corporations. His corporate consulting clients have included giants such as Amway Corporation, Mass Mutual Insurance, Sun Securities, and Weight Watchers International. However, he prefers and mostly works with entrepreneurs who've started and run their own companies.

One of his longest continuing client relationships is with the Guthy-Renker Corporation, famous for its TV infomercials featuring Victoria Principal, Vanessa Williams, Vanna White, and other Hollywood celebrities.

As a consultant to consultants, Dan works closely with more than 50 marketing advisors to different niche industries, with combined impact on well over a million small business owners and self-employed professionals worldwide.

As a direct-response copywriter, Dan creates copy for magazine and newspaper ads, direct-mail campaigns, Web sites, TV infomercials and other media, routinely commanding fees from $20,000.00 to $70,000.00 plus royalties per project. More than 85% of all clients utilizing him as a copywriter once do so repeatedly. You have seen ads he's created for his clients in more than 100 different publications.

Dan is an unusually inaccessible consultant—his office telephones are answered "live" only one afternoon per week; he never takes unscheduled calls, does not carry a cell phone, does not use e-mail, and rarely travels to clients, instead insisting they come to him.

Author

Dan is the author of nine business books in addition to this one, as well as numerous home study courses, audio programs, and other information products. His flagship information product "The Magnetic Marketing System" is the only complete, do-it-yourself direct marketing toolkit for use by any business or sales professional. More than $50 million of these systems have been sold worldwide via Dan's own efforts, the Nightingale-Conant catalog, independent licensed distributors, and as customized editions for certain industries and corporations. A catalog of his authored products is available online at www.dankennedyprod ucts.com.

About the Future

At age 49, Dan announced his semi-retirement and is increasingly selective about the consulting and copywriting projects he will accept. Instead of speaking dozens of times each year at other companies' conferences, Dan now conducts one and only one annual multiday boot camp presenting his most advanced entrepreneurial and marketing strategies, The Renegade Millionaireship Boot Camp. Information is available on line at www.renegademillionaire.com.

After 25 years living in Phoenix, Arizona, and several years of dual residence in Arizona and Ohio, he now lives in northeastern Ohio. He devotes a great deal of time to his large stable of Standardbred racehorses that race there, predominantly at Northfield Park, near Cleveland.

Resource
Directory

This directory will give you information to contact the people and access the resources listed throughout this book. In this directory, you will find many of the people listed chapter by chapter, based on the first reference to them in the book.

Chapter 1

Halbert, Gary. Mentioned here for his statement "Motion beats meditation," Gary is best-known for his legendary prowess as a direct-response ad and direct-mail copywriter, and his marketing newsletter *The Halbert Letter*. Contact: 305-534-7577/Fax 352-861-1665.

Forte, Craig. Publisher of *Service for Life* customer/client newsletters utilized by thousands of real estate agents as well as other types of sales professionals and business owners. Contact: 520-546-1349/Fax 520-546-1359.

Nightingale, Earl. One of the earliest "voices" of modern self-improvement and success education, author of the *Lead the*

Field audio program, and co-founder of Nightingale-Conant Corporation. Today, Nightingale-Conant publishes audio programs by hundreds of leading authors, speakers, and experts ranging from me (Dan Kennedy) to Brian Tracy to Lee Iacocca. Contact: 847-647-0300/Fax 847-647-9243.

Paul, Jeff. Author, *How To Make $4,000.00 a Day Sitting at Home in Your Underwear*, a book about his mail-order/direct marketing experiences that has sold more than 200,000 copies. Contact: 630-778-0018/Fax 630-778-0019.

Milteer, Lee. Author, *Success Is an Inside Job*, speaker, entrepreneurial coach. Lee is a much-sought-after speaker on prosperity, embracing change, and success strategies, with clients including Federal Express, the Disney companies, and NASA. Contact: www.leemilteer.com.

Mancusco, Joe. Founder and president, CEO Clubs, and leading expert on family business matters. CEO (Chief Executive Officer) Clubs operate and welcome members in more than two dozen U.S. cities and host an annual convention and annual management course. Contact: 212-633-0060/Fax 212-633-0063.

LeGrand, Ron. Former "grease monkey" turned outrageously successful real estate investor, Ron now teaches his "Quick Turn-Fast Cash" real estate techniques to thousands of independent investors each year. Contact: 904-262-0491/Fax 904-262-1464, or www.GlobalPublishingInc.com.

Glazer, Bill. Owner, Gage Menswear Stores in Baltimore, Maryland, Bill has become the foremost marketing consultant/coach to the menswear retailing industry. He also publishes marketing systems used by more than 1,500 such retailers as well as thousands more in other niches, including sporting goods, women's apparel, jewelry stores, etc. Bill speaks frequently for associations and at conventions about "Outrageous Advertising for Outrageous Results." Contact: 800-545-0414. Note: Bill is also publisher of Dan Kennedy's *No B.S. Marketing Letter,* information at www.dankennedy.com.

Vance, Michael. Former close confidante and associate of Walt Disney, directly involved in original planning for Epcot, Mike is the most entertaining, fascinating speaker and storyteller in the area of entrepreneurial creativity, and author of *Think Outside The Box.* Contact: 440-243-5576/Fax 440-243-8754.

Snyder, Stephen. Number-one expert on managing credit scores for lowest interest rates. Author, *Credit after Bankruptcy.* Contact: 317-576-0790/Fax 317-596-3710.

Chapter 2

Guthy, Bill; Renker, Greg. Bill and Greg began in TV infomercials with *Think and Grow Rich* featuring Fran Tarkenton in the mid-1980s. Since then, they have led the industry with celebrity-hosted infomercials featuring actresses Victoria Principal, Judith Light, Connie Selleca, Vanessa Williams, and Susan Lucci. They also brought motivational speaker Tony Robbins to television for the first time. Their infomercial-fueled company services millions of continuity customers with skin care, cosmetic, and nutritional products. Contact: Guthy-Renker Corporation, Palm Desert, California.

Polish, Joe. President, Piranha Marketing ("Eat Your Competition Alive!"), Joe provides nearly 5,000 carpet cleaning business owners with advertising and marketing systems, Web sites, customer newsletters, training, and an annual conference. More than 100 business owners pay $10,000.00 each per year to participate in his coaching program. Contact: 480-858-0008/Fax 480-858-0004, or www.joepolish.com.

Chapter 3

Hoisington, Reed. Coach, trainer, provider of marketing systems and seminars to mortgage brokers nationwide. Reed's company also provides fax, direct-mail, and telephone marketing services for mortgage companies, generating hundreds of millions of dollars of mortgage revenues each year. Contact: 910-484-4519/Fax 910-485-3524.

Chapter 4

Fatt, Rory. President, Restaurant Marketing Systems Inc. Rory provides thousands of restaurant owners with advertising and marketing systems, Web sites, customer newsletters, training, and an annual conference. Contact: 604-940-6900/Fax 604-940-6902.

Storms, Mike. Owner, Mike Storms Karate, Mandeville, Louisiana; author, "Safer, Smarter Kids Program" taught nationally; and provider of marketing systems and seminars to martial arts school owners nationwide. Mike is best-known in marketing circles for the astoundingly sophisticated, 21-step system for stimulating maximum referrals originally implemented in his own school, since "genericized" and taught to business owners in many fields as well as chiropractors and dentists. Mike is available for speaking engagements with business and sales groups. Contact: 985-674-7887/Fax 985-674-3595.

Chapter 5

Proctor, Craig. Year after year, Craig is in the top ten RE/MAX real estate agents worldwide yet operates his agent business part-time—an achievement possible because of his unique, well-oiled marketing machine cloned and taught to more than 10,000 other agents via his coaching programs and seminars. Contact: 905-853-6135/Fax 905-853-6078.

Chapter 6

Scheinfeld, Robert. Author, *The Invisible Path.* Bob has repeatedly engineered dramatic, rapid value growth in companies, most recently selling the software company he built to Intuit for $177 million. His grandfather Aaron Scheinfeld started and built Manpower, Inc. Today, Bob offers comprehensive training and coaching for entrepreneurs encompassing a wide range of skills, from intuitive innovation to success without sacrifice of lifestyle. Contact: 434-984-3235/Fax 703-637-1301.

Yellen, Pamela. President, Prospecting and Marketing Institute, a revolutionary force in the life insurance industry. Co-author with Dan Kennedy, *Zero Resistance Selling,* the only sales book based on Dr. Maxwell Maltz's Psycho-Cybernetics. Contact: 505-466-1167/Fax 505-466-2167.

Furey, Matt. Author, *Combat Conditioning,* and popular author, coach and seminar leader in health, fitness, martial arts, and anti-aging. As an entrepreneur, Matt has achieved extraordinary success marketing a variety of information products via the Internet and conducts "boot camps" teaching Internet marketing, publishing, and entrepreneurship. Contact: 813-994-8267/Fax 813-994-4947. Note: Matt is also the master-licensee and publisher of the Psycho-Cybernetics Foundation's courses. www.psycho-cybernetics.com.

Sugarman, Joe. Author, *Advertising Secrets of the Written Word* and *Triggers.* Joe was the first advertiser to offer credit card ordering via a toll-free 800-number and is a legendary pioneer of countless other marketing strategies and innovations. Joe is available for speaking engagements. Contact: Fax 702-597-2002.

Abraham, Jay. Author, *Getting Everything You Can Out of Everything You've Got.* Jay is famous for uncovering hidden and unexploited opportunities in businesses big and small, with clients including IBM, Microsoft, Citibank, and Charles Schwab. Contact: www.abraham.com.

Kimble, Michael. President, Group-M Publishing. Group-M publishes a variety of how-to products for sales professionals, small-business owners, and direct marketers, and is the exclusive worldwide publisher of more than 50 Dan Kennedy programs. Contact: 512-263-2299/Fax 512-263-9898, or www.kimble-kennedypublishing.com or www.dankennedyproducts.com.

Chapter 7

Ziglar, Zig. One of America's most popular, celebrated motivational speakers for three generations, Zig's book *See You at the Top* is a true classic. Contact: www.zigziglar.com.

Rowland, Chet. Chet provides thousands of pest control business owners with advertising and marketing systems, Web sites, customer newsletters, training, seminars, and field trips to his pest control company and "Chetland" in Tampa, Florida. Contact: 888-444-0442/Fax 813-932-5642.

Chapter 9

Reed, William. Lawyer turned consumer/entrepreneur advocate, author, *Bullet Proof Asset Protection.* Contact: Asset Protection Group, Las Vegas, Nevada.

Altadonna, Ben (Dr.). Ben provides thousands of chiropractors with advertising and marketing systems, Web sites, customer newsletters, training, and seminars. Contact: 925-314-9669/Fax 925-891-3851.

Chapter 10

Nathan, Lester. Leading consultant to independent pharmacy owners on prospering against Goliath competition, profit improvement, and staff issues. Contact: 518-346-7021/Fax 518-346-8325.

Geier, Jay. Jay's proprietary system for improving staff handling of inbound calls from prospects, customers, clients, and patients is dramatically improving profits in thousands of diverse businesses, and he is available to speak on the subject. His Scheduling Institute of America provides training to staff members in the chiropractic, dental, cosmetic surgery, and other health-related professions. Contact: 888-993-2855.

Chapter 12

Carlton, John. One of the great iconoclasts among top, professional ad/direct-response copywriters, John also frequently speaks at seminars and publishes a newsletter on marketing. Contact: 775-624-6224/Fax 775-562-2655.

Chapter 13

Maltz, Maxwell. The late Dr. Maltz was the father of "self-image psychology," and his original book *Psycho-Cybernetics* has sold more than 30 million copies worldwide. Dan Kennedy and several associates acquired all rights to all Dr. Maltz works, and in recent years, Kennedy has co-authored *The New Psycho-Cybernetics* book, *The New Psycho-Cybernetics* audio program by Nightingale-Conant, and the *Zero Resistance Selling* book. Psycho-Cybernetics is, in essence, a scientific approach with practical mental training techniques to improve all aspects of personal performance. Info at www.psycho-cybernetics.com.

Chapter 15

Jones, Jerry. Publisher, *Healthy, Wealthy, Wise* patient/customer newsletter, provider of direct-mail and Web-based marketing services primarily to the dental profession. Contact: 503-371-1390/Fax 503-371-1299.

Chapter 18

Rudl, Corey. Corey has developed some of the most sophisticated software programs and online services for conducting e-commerce and e-publishing. He is the author of *Insider Secrets to E-Mail Marketing.* Contact: 604-730-2833/Fax 604-638-6015.

Silver, Yanik. Another "guru" of Internet marketing, Yanik has authored numerous e-books, books, and courses; frequently speaks at seminars and conferences; conducts coaching programs; and has a number of member-restricted Web sites providing business tools such as instant sales letters. Contact: 301-770-0423/Fax 301-770-1096, and www.surefiremarketing.com.

Romano, Ron. President, Automated Marketing Solutions. Provides 800-number recorded message, lead capture, broadcast fax, broadcast voice, and other technology services. Contact: 800-858-8889/Fax 800-858-5753, and www.findmeleads.com.

Chapter 19

Nielsen, Louise. Cleaning Concepts Unlimited, 7914 W. Dodge Rd. #391, Omaha, Nebraska 68114.

Garman, Darrin. Iowa Realty, Commercial Real Estate Marketing. Contact: 319-378-6748/Fax 319-373-5535.

Other Books by the Author

Ultimate Marketing Plan (Adams Media)

Ultimate Sales Letter (Adams Media)

NO RULES: 21 Giant Lies About Success (Plume)

How To Make Millions with Your Ideas (Plume)

The New Psycho-Cybernetics (Prentice-Hall)

Zero Resistance Selling (Prentice Hall)

No B.S. Sales Success (Entrepreneur Press)

No B.S. Time Management for Entrepreneurs (Entrepreneur Press)

Author's Web Sites

www.dankennedy.com

www.dankennedyproducts.com

www.renegademillionaire.com

www.psycho-cybernetics.com

To Contact the Author Directly

Phone: 602-997-7707

Fax: 602-269-3113

Eternal Truths

Dan Kennedy's Eternal Truth #1

Every successful achievement begins with decision. Most unsuccessful lives are conspicuously absent of decision.

• • • • •

Dan Kennedy's Eternal Truth #2

If it's work, it won't make you rich.

• • • • •

Dan Kennedy's Eternal Truth #3

Failure is part of the daily entrepreneurial experience.

• • • • •

Dan Kennedy's Eternal Truth #4

How you deal with failure determines whether or not you ever get the opportunity to deal with success.

• • • • •

Dan Kennedy's Eternal Truth #5

You cannot trust your own judgment. Test, test, test. Then test some more.

• • • • •

Dan Kennedy's Eternal Truth #6

Live by price, die by price.

• • • • •

Dan Kennedy's Eternal Truth #7

We're taught that you can't judge a book by its cover, but we can't help but judge a book by its cover. You will be judged that way, too.

• • • • •

Dan Kennedy's Eternal Truth #8

No one will ever be a bigger expert on your business than you.

• • • • •

Dan Kennedy's Eternal Truth #9

The willingness to do whatever it takes is infinitely more important than knowing everything there is to know about how to do it.

• • • • •

Dan Kennedy's Eternal Truth #10

The ability to win is easily transferred from one business to another.

• • • • •

Dan Kennedy's Eternal Truth #11

Talk is cheap . . . until you hire a lawyer.

• • • • •

Dan Kennedy's Eternal Truth #12

No one will ever care about your business as much as you do.

• • • • •

Dan Kennedy's Eternal Truth #13

Cash is king.

• • • • •

Dan Kennedy's Eternal Truth #14

If you can't make money without money, you probably can't make money with money either.

• • • • •

Dan Kennedy's Eternal Truth #15

There is never enough time (or enough of any other resource, for that matter). Entrepreneurs learn to get what they want working with what they've got.

• • • • •

Dan Kennedy's Eternal Truth #16

Even a blind hog finds a truffle once in a while—as long as it keeps poking around.

• • • • •

Dan Kennedy's Eternal Truth #17

No one on his deathbed says: "I wish I'd spent more time at the office." Not even a true entrepreneur.

• • • • •

Dan Kennedy's Eternal Truth #18

What goes around, comes around.

• • • • •

Dan Kennedy's Eternal Truth #19

A "normal" small-business can only yield a "normal" small-business income. To earn an extraordinary income, you must develop an extraordinary business!

• • • • •

Dan Kennedy's Eternal Truth #20

Passion wanes with longevity and familiarity.

• • • • •

Dan Kennedy's Eternal Truth #21

When you're up to your neck in alligators, it's difficult to remember that your original objective was to drain the swamp.

Preface to

No B.S. Sales Success

There are basically four types of salespeople: sales professionals with strong ambition who are eager to strengthen and fine-tune their skills; sales professionals who are jaded, close-minded, cynical, and stuck; nonsalespeople who realize they need to be, such as doctors, auto repair shop owners, carpet cleaners; and nonsalespeople who either do not recognize they need to be or are resistant to the idea.

Ambitious Salespeople 1	Stuck Salespeople 2
3 Nonsalespeople Eager to Learn	4 Resistant Nonsalespeople

This book will resonate with those in the first and third quadrant. It will be wasted on the others. I've spent more than one-fourth of an entire lifetime, more than 25 years, working with people in both the first and third quadrant—and doing my level best to avoid the folks in the second and fourth. This book literally summarizes the most important strategies I've developed over those 25 years—some originating from my own experience, others originating from my observation of super-successful sales pros' behaviors that I have converted to replicatable strategy.

There are a great many things this book is NOT. It is NOT, for example, a textbook approach to selling. It is not about moral or spiritual philosophy (those matters are left to you). It is only slightly about the psychology of selling. It is noticeably free of trendy new terminology, buzzwords, and psycho-babble so many sales trainers and authors seem to be fond of. And it is not a motivational book either. If you need someone else to motivate you, you have far bigger problems than this book might tackle. Or any hundred books, for that matter.

This is simply a straightforward, relentlessly pragmatic, "no b.s." *presentation of what REALLY works in selling.* Not what should work. Not the academic theories about selling. What REALLY works.

You may not thoroughly enjoy this book. It may make you uncomfortable. Confronting, challenging, and rethinking long-held beliefs and habits is provocative and often profitable but rarely comfortable or enjoyable.

My aim is very simple: after reading this book, I intend for you to implement behavioral and procedural changes that will immediately and dramatically increase the income you earn from selling. This book is all about putting more money in your pocket, nothing loftier than that, nothing less than that. And if we have to break a few eggs to make that omelet, then that's what we'll do.

You might want to know that this book has had a long former life. It was first published in 1994, has been in print continuously through 1996, a 2nd edition was published in 1999, which was in print through 2001, and now this thoroughly updated and substantially expanded in this new edition. Why is it important for you to know you've wound up with "the sales book that will not die" in your hands? Two reasons. First, as evidence you've gotten your paws on strategies that ARE really valuable and that DO really work. Successful salespeople recommend this book to each other, they stream to the bookstores and demand it. Even when a publisher has lost interest in it, the marketplace has insisted this book be put back onto the store shelves. (By the way, now you can tell others about this book by sending them to www.nobsbooks. com, to get free excerpts.) Second, you will see references in the book that are obviously dated, or references to my writing of its first edition, and I didn't want you to be confused by that; thus, this explanation.

Now, to the important stuff: quick, practical actions you can take to make selling easier, less stressful, more fun, and much, much more lucrative and rewarding.

About the Structure of This Book

This book is divided into six parts. In Part 1, I describe the 15 strategies I use most in selling. Each is a stand-alone application, and any one of them alone could significantly improve your results in selling. But they can also be linked together differently for different situations for increased value and power.

In Part 2, I deal with what goes on before selling can even begin: finding, attracting, and getting into a selling situation with a prospect. As you'll see, I'm no fan of the way most salespeople carry out this job. Here you'll discover some rather radical ideas.

In Part 3, I provide a framework for selling. The various pieces described in Parts 1 and 2 can be plugged in and out of this structure.

In Part 4, I share with you the dumbest things salespeople do to sabotage themselves.

In Part 5, I reveal my personal, best, most valued, contrary approach to selling. It may not be for everybody; it may not be for you. Frankly, I argued with myself about putting it in or leaving it out. I ultimately decided I would not be playing fair with you if I sold you a book about selling and held back the information most responsible for my own success. Use it as you will, and good luck.

In the last decade, the sales world has been flooded with new technology, and Part 6 of this edition contains an updated section on my "no b.s." observations of this.

—Dan S. Kennedy

Preface to

No B.S. Time Management
for Entrepreneurs

It gets late early out here.

—Yogi Berra

Wimps and Willie Lomans—beware! This book is not for the faint of heart, fawningly polite, or desperate to be liked.

Hopefully, you have picked up this book because you are an entrepreneur, your time is incredibly valuable to you, and you are constantly "running out of it."

If you know me, then you've also been motivated to get this book to find out how I manage to do all that I do. I have been asked so often, by, what seems like everybody who becomes familiar with my life, how the devil I fit it all in, that I sat down and wrote out the answer—this book. If you don't know me, then your curiosity about my methods may be further piqued by the description of my activities that follow this Preface. If you know me, skip that section.

As a very busy, sometimes frantic, time-pressured entrepreneur, awash in opportunity, too often surrounded by nitwits and slower-than-molasses-pouring-uphill folk, I understand your needs, desires, and frustrations. The multiple demands on an entrepreneur's time are *extraordinary*. So I am here to tell you that you need to take extraordinary measures to match those demands. Measures so radical and extreme that others may question your sanity. This is no ordinary time management book for the deskbound or the person doing just one job. This book is expressly for the wearer of many hats, the inventive, opportunistic entrepreneur who can't resist piling more and more responsibility onto his own shoulders, who has many more great ideas than time and resources to take advantage of them, who runs (not walks) through each day. I'm you, and this is our book.

As you have undoubtedly discovered, time is the most precious asset any entrepreneur possesses. Time to solve problems. Time to invent, create, think, and plan. Time to gather and assimilate information. Time to develop sales, marketing, management, and profit breakthroughs. Time to network. Probably not a day goes by that you don't shove something aside, sigh, and say to yourself: *"If I could only find an extra hour* to work on this, it'd make a huge difference in our business." Well, I'm going to give you that extra hour. But what we're about to do here together is much bigger than just eking out an extra hour here or there. We are going to drastically re-engineer your entire relationship with time.

I've had more than 25 plus years of high-pressure, high-wire-without-a-net entrepreneurial activity—starting, buying, developing, selling, succeeding in and failing in businesses, going broke, getting profoundly rich, and helping clients in hundreds of different fields. Here's what I've come to believe to be the single biggest "secret" of extraordinary personal, financial, and entrepreneurial success combined: the use or misuse (or abuse by others) of your time—the degree to which you achieve peak productivity—will determine your success. So this book is about everything that can be done to achieve peak personal productivity.

Just thinking about it is a big step in the right direction. Awareness helps a lot. There's a reason why you can't find a wall clock in a casino to save your life—those folks stealing your money do not want you to be aware of the passing of time. And that tells you something useful right there: you want to be very aware, all the time, of the passing of time. It is to your advantage to be very conscious of the passage and usage of minutes and hours. Put a good, big, easily visible, "nagging" clock in every work area. If you spend a lot of time on the phone, have and use a timer.

Beyond simple awareness, there are practical strategies, methods, procedures, and tools that the busiest, most pressured person can use to crowbar some breathing room into his schedule, to force others to cooperate with his exceptional needs, to squeeze just a bit more out of each day. In this book, I give you mine. You will undoubtedly be interested in some, disinterested in others, maybe even repulsed by a few. That's OK. Although it's generally a bad idea to hire an advice-giver and then choose only the advice you like, in this case, it IS a cafeteria, and you can pick and choose and still get value.

Now it is time to get to work.

—Dan S. Kennedy

Index

Special Free Gift #1 from the Author
FREE
$138.90 Value Kennedy Information Package

Special Reports

1. **21 Tough, No B.S. Questions Every Entrepreneur Needs.** Throughout this book, smart questions have been raised. Every entrepreneur needs an arsenal of tough questions—to ask himself, to ask his associates, to ask his vendors. This report includes some from the book plus many not in the book, compiled from various Dan Kennedy sources, including past one-time-only seminars like his "Ultimate Marketing and Entrepreneurship/Lifetime of Secrets Boot Camp." (Sold separately for $49.95.)

2. **Inside Secrets of Kennedy Consulting: How Clients' Sales and Profits Are Multiplied, Problems Solved.** A collection of articles, case histories, and examples from past issues of Dan's *No B.S. Marketing Letter,* as well as case history examples from client files (used with permission) assembled exclusively for this report. You will see examples of uncovering hidden or neglected profit opportunities, successfully raising prices and selling at prices higher than competitors, surviving business crises, and more. (Sold separately for $49.95.)

3. **Renegade Millionaire System Preview Audio Presentation.** Two audio presentations, one an overview and introduction to Dan's "Renegade Millionaire System"—the blueprint for doing business successfully entirely on your terms; the second, highlights of interviews with "Renegade Millionaires." ($39.00 value.)

To Obtain this Free Information Package: There is no need to damage your book by tearing out this Coupon—a photocopy is satisfactory. Complete ALL the information required, then either fax this form to 410-727-0978 or mail to Glazer-Kennedy Inner Circle, 200 W. Baltimore St., Baltimore, MD 21201. Allow 2 to 3 weeks for delivery. Providing information below constitutes permission for Glazer-Kennedy Inner Circle to contact you with information about its products and services.

Name _____ Business name _____

Address _____ ❏ Business ❏ Home

City/state/zip_____ E-mail _____

Phone _____ Fax _____

E-mail address _____

FREE

Test Drive Three-Months of Dan Kennedy's
"Elite" Gold Inner Circle Membership

Receive a steady stream of marketing and business building advice

Yes Dan, I want to take you up on your offer of a FREE Three-Month Gold Inner Circle Membership, which includes:

1. Three months of your *No B.S. Marketing Newsletter*
2. Three months of your Exclusive Audiocassette Interviews
3. Three months of your Marketing Gold Hotsheet
4. Special FREE Gold Member Call-In Times
5. Gold Member Restricted Access Web Site
6. Continually updated Million Dollar Resource Directory
7. Open fax line
8. At least a 30% discount to future Glazer-Kennedy events and seminars

There is a one-time charge of $5.95 to cover postage for ALL three months of the FREE Gold Membership, and you have no obligation to continue at the *lowest* Gold Member price of $39.97 per month ($49.97 outside North America). In fact, should you continue with membership, you can cancel at any time by calling Glazer-Kennedy Inner Circle at 410-951-0147 or faxing a cancellation note to 410-727-0978.

Name _____ Business name _____

Address _____ ❑ Business ❑ Home

City/state/zip_____ E-mail _____

Phone _____ Fax _____

Credit card   ❑ Visa   ❑ MasterCard   ❑ American Express

Credit card number _____ Exp date _____

Signature_____ Date _____

Providing this information constitutes your permission for Glazer-Kennedy Inner Circle LLC to contact you regarding related information via mail, e-mail, fax, and phone.